YOU KNOW, YOU CAN, YOU WILL

Napoleon Hill (1883–1970), best known for his global bestseller *Think and Grow Rich*, was a self-help author and businessman whose work has influenced millions across the world, from Norman Vincent Peale to Donald Trump. Born poor, Hill lived a colourful life, pursuing several different business ventures and professions. He also met and advised many famous people, such as US President Woodrow Wilson. Hill eventually found widespread success as a motivational author, writing several books on how to achieve success and practically creating the self-help genre.

YOU KNOW, YOU CAN, YOU WILL

Success Lessons for Life

NAPOLEON HILL

Published by
Rupa Publications India Pvt. Ltd 2024
7/16, Ansari Road, Daryaganj
New Delhi 110002

Sales centres:
Bengaluru Chennai
Hyderabad Jaipur Kathmandu
Kolkata Mumbai Prayagraj

Edition copyright © Rupa Publications India Pvt. Ltd 2024

All rights reserved.
No part of this publication may be reproduced, transmitted,
or stored in a retrieval system, in any form or by any means, electronic,
mechanical, photocopying, recording or otherwise, without the prior
permission of the publisher.

P-ISBN: 978-93-5702-896-7
E-ISBN: 978-93-5702-894-3

First impression 2024

10 9 8 7 6 5 4 3 2 1

Printed in India

This book is sold subject to the condition that it shall not, by way of
trade or otherwise, be lent, resold, hired out, or otherwise circulated,
without the publisher's prior consent, in any form of binding or
cover other than that in which it is published.

CONTENTS

1. The Limitless Power of the Mind — 7
2. Specialized Knowledge — 30
3. Organized Thought — 40
4. A Definite Chief Aim — 56
5. Initiative and Leadership — 63
6. Go the Extra Mile — 69
7. Failure May Be a Blessing — 89
8. Learn to See — 97
9. Self-Confidence — 112
10. How to Find Satisfaction in Your Job — 135
11. The 17 Principles of Success — 148

1

THE LIMITLESS POWER OF THE MIND

The mind of man would lead all the other Miracles of Life if they had been described in the order of their importance, because the mind is the instrument through which man relates himself to all things and circumstances that affect or influence his life.

Without doubt the human mind is the most mysterious, the most awe-inspiring product which nature has produced, and at the same time it is the least understood, and the most often abused, of man's profound gifts from the Creator.

The mind is the citadel of the soul, wherein is housed the connecting link between the conscious thinking process of man and Infinite Intelligence. It is the switchboard, so to speak, through which man may tune in and communicate directly with the great universal reservoir of Infinite Intelligence, and draw therefrom the answers to all his problems, the way of fulfillment of all his hopes, dreams, and aspirations.

And most profound of all, *the mind is the one and only thing over which the Creator has given man the complete right of control; a prerogative which not even the Creator has set aside, reversed, or in any manner usurped, which strongly suggests that the mind was intended for man's exclusive use; that it is the most important of all the gifts of the Creator; and the means by which man may control the major portion of his earthly destiny.*

All of man's successes and all of his failures and frustrations are the direct result of the manner in which he uses his mind, *or neglects to use it.*

The functional operations of the mind are divided into nine departments, something on the order of a well-organized business. Some of these departments function automatically, without direction by the individual, while other departments *are under the control of the individual at all times.*

Here is a breakdown of all the departments of the mind:

(a) The Faculty of Will: The Will is the "big boss" of all the other departments of the mind. Here is the starting point where the individual begins to exercise his Great Prerogative privilege of *exclusive control over his thoughts.* The faculty of the Will is the "yes" and the "no" man of the entire mind. It carries out orders of the individual, regardless of their nature or the effect they may have upon the individual. The power of the Will remains strong in exact proportion to its use. An idle Will, like an idle arm, will become soft and weak.

(b) The Faculty of Reason: The faculty of Reason is the "presiding judge" of the mind. When directed, or permitted, to do so, it will pass judgment on all ideas, aims, desires, purposes, and circumstances which the individual brings to its attention; but its decisions can be set aside by the "big boss," the Will, or offset by the influence of the emotions if the Will does not assert itself. One of the major weaknesses of all so-called thinking is the tendency of individuals to allow their Wills to be set aside by their emotions. This error can be, and it often is, tragic, because the emotions have no relation to logic or reason; therefore, all action growing out of the emotions should have careful attention of the Will.

(c) The Faculty of Emotions: Here is the starting place of a major portion of all actions of the mind. People make decisions which harmonize with their "feelings," and engage in activities which have not been previewed by the faculties of Reason and Will. Such decisions are more often unsound than sound.

The most common reckless use of the emotions, without due attention from the faculties of Reason and Will, originates through the emotion of Love. The emotion of Love partakes of a spiritual quality of the highest order, but it may be, and it often is, the most dangerous of all the emotions because people generally do not submit it to the modifying influence of the Reason and the Will.

Accurate thinkers—people who use all the departments of their minds in the process of thinking—never allow the emotion of Love to express itself until its actions have been carefully looked over by the Reason and the Will. Moreover, the accurate thinker submits all of his deepest desires, plans, and purposes to his departments of Reason and Will *to make sure that his eagerness and enthusiasm do not overthrow his Wisdom*; and his emotion of Love is always under constant suspicion lest it get from under his control.

(d) The Faculty of Imagination: This faculty is the architect of man's soul through which he may pattern his own earthly destiny to suit himself and change or modify that pattern as often as he pleases. With the aid of his Imagination, man may penetrate the interstellar spaces of infinitude with the speed of lightning, conquer the air above him and the seas below him, and create a million ideas and concepts of benefit to himself by merely combining in new ways old ideas and concepts.

Through his Imagination man may combine fantasy with realism and shape these into living empires of industry which change the entire trend of civilization. Nothing is impossible of accomplishment by the Imagination which is guided by the faculties of Will and Reason, but *unbridled Imagination can play havoc with an individual's life;* and it has been said that when the emotion of Love and the Imagination get together and go on an unchaperoned spree, the individual may never recover from the damage they do.

The Imagination is the place of origin of the sixty-four dollar physical ailment known as hypochondria, which has proved to be a major problem with doctors. It may also be the place of origin of the cure for hypochondria, and there are many reliable authorities who claim that the Imagination exercises such powerful influence over the physical body that it can activate the body resistance mechanism and cause it to eliminate many types of real physical ailments.

The Imagination is a great institution whose *potentialities are practically unlimited, but it is a very tricky institution which requires constant supervision by the faculties of the Reason and the Will.* It may be helpful if you will read the preceding sentence many times, until you become impressed by the potency of the suggestion it carries.

(e) The Faculty of Conscience: Here we have the department of the mind which gives moral guidance to the individual. If allowed to function without interference, the Conscience carefully processes all of the individual's aims and purposes and warns him when they do not harmonize with the moral laws of nature. This warning ceases and the Conscience eventually goes out of business altogether *if the individual fails or neglects to heed its warnings.*

The individual who has the full support of his Conscience in connection with all his desires, aims and purposes, has direct access to the necessary Faith to enable him to accomplish whatever he may set his heart and mind upon.

(f) The Five Physical Senses: The five senses—sight, sound, taste, smell and touch—are the physical "arms" of the brain, through which it contacts the external world and acquires information. The senses are not always reliable; therefore, they require constant supervision by the faculties of Reason and Will.

Under any sort of highly emotional activity, the senses often become confused and highly undependable, as in the case of sudden fright, or intense anger. No decision which is reached under the influence of fear or anger should be allowed to stand, until it has been thoroughly reviewed by Will and Reason.

(g) The Faculty of Memory: Here is the "filing cabinet" of the brain wherein is stored all thought impulses, all conscious experiences, and all sensations which reach the brain through the five physical senses. The Memory is also very undependable, as most individuals can testify. Therefore, it needs supervision and discipline by the Will and the Reason. The main cause for the unreliability of the Memory is due to the fact that the "filing clerk"—the individual who supervises the action of the Memory—is careless in not having a definite system by which to work.

The Memory can be made reasonably reliable with the aid of a practical Memory training course, such as the Roth system. Reliability of the Memory is entirely a matter of discipline, supervision, and education of the "filing clerk" who is responsible for the function of this important faculty of the mind.

(h) The "Sixth Sense": This is the broadcasting and the receiving station of the mind through which one automatically sends and receives vibrations of thought, and perhaps other still higher vibrations which emanate on planes of intelligence outside that of our own earth. This is the medium of communication between the individual and the Unseen Guides which are believed to be available for his service.

The "Sixth Sense" is the medium through which a properly qualified mind may communicate with other minds, at any distance, through the principle of telepathy. The principle of telepathy has been recognized, by reliable authorities, as a workable reality, and the means by which it may be put into service has been described in detail in many books, including some which I have written.

(i) The Subconscious Section of the Mind: This is the "switchboard" through which the conscious section of the mind may communicate directly with Infinite Intelligence. The Subconscious acts upon any idea, plan, or purpose which reaches it, and it makes no attempt to distinguish the difference between positive and negative, or right or wrong influences. But it does respond more quickly and effectively to influences which have been highly emotionalized with such emotions as fear, anger, *belief*, and *faith*.

The Subconscious section of the mind is amenable to the influences of the conscious section of the mind, which often stubbornly closes the door to the Subconscious through fears and limitations and false beliefs. In order to get around these negative barricades set up by the conscious section of the mind, and in order to give directions to the Subconscious for the cure of physical ailments, doctors of Suggestive Therapeutics often wait until the individual is asleep (sometimes through hypnotism) and then communicate directly with the Subconscious.

As stated earlier, there is a machine in successful operation with which any desired order can be given to the Subconscious while the individual is asleep. The orders or instructions are recorded on a phonograph record and placed on the machine which plays them every fifteen minutes (until the individual awakes and turns off the machine). The machine is operated by a clock which can be set to start the playing of the record after the individual is asleep.

The references in this volume to the departments of the mind are, of necessity, brief and not intended as exhaustive analyses of these subjects, but merely a bird's-eye picture of the "mechanism" through which the human mind operates, together with a brief description of the extent to which the departments of the mind are under the control of the individual.

We would emphasize that all thought, whether it is negative or positive, sound or unsound, tends to clothe itself in its physical equivalent, and it proceeds to do so by inspiring the individual with ideas, plans, and purposes for the attainment of desired ends, through natural and logical means. After thought on any subject becomes, through repetition, a habit, it is taken over and automatically acted upon by the Subconscious.

It may not be true that "thoughts are things," but it is true that thoughts create things, and the things thus created are strikingly similar to the nature of the thoughts from which they are fashioned.

It is believed by many people, who are competent to judge accurately, that every thought which one releases starts an unending vibration with which the one who releases it will have to contend later; that man himself is but the physical reflection of thought put into motion by Infinite Intelligence. It is also the belief of many that the energy with which people think is but a projected portion of Infinite Intelligence which the individual appropriates from the universal source, through the equipment of the brain.

We have now reached the point at which we shall begin the explanation of the means by which one's mind may be conditioned for dentistry, major surgical operations, or any other unpleasant experience which one may have to face.

The *conditioning* of the mind must be done entirely through the subconscious section of the mind. Therefore, let us have a further look at the means by which the subconscious may be reached and directed to any desired end at will.

You cannot *entirely control* your subconscious mind, but you can voluntarily influence it to act upon any desire, plan, or purpose which you may wish translated into concrete form.

The subconscious never remains idle. If you neglect to keep it busy with desires of your own choice it will feed upon the thoughts inspired by your environment, especially those associated with the things you do not want, the things you fear or dislike.

Whether you recognize it or not, you are living daily in the midst of all sorts of thought impulses which are reaching your subconscious mind without your knowledge. Some of these impulses are negative; some are positive. You are now about to be informed how to shut off the flow of negative influences which reach and influence you, and the means by which these negative influences, including all fears, may be supplanted by desires, plans, and purposes *of your own choosing*, including, in particular, the means of mastering physical pain.

When you master the technique you are about to receive, and learn to apply it, you will possess the key which unlocks the door to your subconscious mind, *and you will control that door so completely that no undesirable thoughts or influences can pass through it.*

Before we describe the method of approach to the subconscious mind you should recognize that there are two doors to your subconscious. One door opens outward toward the physical world in which you live, and that world can be entered only through that door. *The other door opens inwardly and connects directly with the great universal reservoir of Infinite Intelligence* .

It is through these two doors that prayer operates.

It is through these two doors that one's hopes, desires, and plans may be fulfilled through *definiteness of purpose* and a *burning desire* for its realization.

It is through these two doors that all of one's fears, doubts, and discouragements are translated into the miseries of life *if the conscious mind is allowed to dwell upon these undesirable conditions*. Every thought one sends to the subconscious mind; every thought which reaches the subconscious mind because of one's neglect to process and reject negative thoughts inspired by one's environment, is automatically accepted by the subconscious and acted upon.

One of the greatest of the inconsistencies of mankind is the fact that the majority of people go through life with their minds devoted largely to thinking of all the things and circumstances *they do not wish*—poverty, failure, ill health, unhappiness, and physical pain— and they then wonder why they are cursed with all of these undesirable conditions.

The mind attracts to one the exact material equivalent of that which one thinks about most often. Along with this statement of fact, remember that the Creator provided every normal person with complete, unchallengeable right and power to control and direct his mind power to whatever ends he may choose, and you will have no difficulty in recognizing that *all undesirable circumstances one meets with are the results of neglect to take possession of the mind and to guide it to the ends one desires.*

HYPOCHONDRIA, THE DOCTOR'S $64.00 WORD

Hypochondria means *imaginary* physical ailment! It is a conservative statement to say that this ailment gives doctors and dentists more trouble than all the real ailments known to mankind. The fear of ill health, and its first cousin, the fear of physical pain, are inherited states of mind, and they constitute one of the Seven Basic Fears with which all people suffer at one time or another.

In my public lectures some years ago, I gave dramatic demonstrations of the nature of this inborn fear of ill health, and of physical pain—demonstrations which proved that persons with not a single trace of physical ailments could be made violently ill by mere suggestion.

The technique by which this was demonstrated was very simple. With the aid of four assistants, who were stationed secretly at various places in and out of the auditorium where I was lecturing, the demonstration was carried out. A "victim" was secretly chosen from the audience by a committee of my students. At recess, by prearrangement with my "stooges," each of them approached the "victim" and asked him or her questions.

Stooge number one would ask, "Are you not feeling well? You look as if you are ill." Stooge number two would rush up to the "victim" and in an excited voice exclaim, "I say, my friend, you look as if you are about to faint! Can I get you a drink of water?" Stooge number three would soon appear and say to the victim, "Let me give you a hand. You look as if you are about to pass out." Then, turning to those who were looking on, he would add: "Here, folks, help me find a place for this person to lie down. He is ill."

If the "victim" had not actually passed out by this time,

he generally did so when the fourth stooge approached him, grabbed him by the arm, and called, "Someone call a doctor quickly. This person needs attention."

I performed this experiment many times and never failed to make the "victim" temporarily ill. Finally the person chosen for the experiment, a man about thirty years of age, so completely passed out that he had to be hospitalized for a short time. The doctors finally convinced him that he had been the victim of an experimental hoax.

After that experience I tried no more experiments of this nature.

Convince the subconscious mind that you are ill, and it will go to work immediately to carry that conviction to its logical conclusion by actually making you ill. Hypochondria often produces the actual physical symptoms of illness, such as the breaking out of rash, or an upset stomach, or a headache, when the actual cause is nothing more than fear.

Inmates of the Ohio State Penitentiary formerly played a cruel joke on many of the newcomers to prison. The joke consisted of a committee of prisoners charging the newcomer with some imaginary infraction of the prison rules, and then condemning him to death. The victim was then blindfolded; his hands were tied behind him and his head was placed over a barrel, with several men holding him down tightly. Then one of the gang would ask if the knife had been properly sharpened. Someone would say, "Yes, I sharpened it myself right after we killed that last man. Here it is—now let him have it good and hard so he can't scream."

With that part of the ceremony finished, a comb would be roughly drawn across the victim's neck, quickly followed by spilling red ink over the neck. Then the victim would be turned loose, and everyone else would run for cover. Generally the first thing the victim did was to pull the blindfold from his eyes, and rub his neck with his hands, which of course led him to believe his throat had been cut, because there was the "blood" on his hands.

On one occasion a man thus victimized was so badly scared that he started running and screaming that he had been murdered. He had to be caught and subdued by prison guards, after which he was hospitalized for several days before he recovered from the shock, despite the fact he could plainly see his throat had not been cut.

The fear of sickness and the fear of physical pain are inborn fears, which come to the surface and take over at the slightest provocation. The fear itself, however, is always much worse than the thing which is feared. As Franklin D. Roosevelt said, during his first term in office, when the country was cursed by a stampede of fear, "The only thing we have to fear is FEAR itself." The truth might well be paraphrased in connection with the fear of dentistry, because modern dental techniques have practically removed all physical pain from every portion of the patient's body except one, *and that is the brain where his fear of pain exists, as a condition of mind he has created long before he sits in the dentist's chair.*

HOW TO REACH AND INFLUENCE THE SUBCONSCIOUS MIND

The subconscious section of the mind receives activating influences from three sources: First, from all outside sources which convey influences to the individual through the five physical senses, including of course the words and deeds of others which come to one's attention. Second, through the sixth sense, which picks up thoughts released by others and passes them on to the individual by telepathy. Third, from the thoughts of the individual, including both the thoughts which are deliberately sent to the subconscious in the form of aims, plans, or desires, and *random thoughts which the individual indulges in without particular plan or purpose.*

Random, careless, negative thoughts occupy the minds of most people, and such thoughts produce undesirable circumstances, because they are picked up by the subconscious and acted upon. The subconscious does not differentiate between negative and positive thoughts, but accepts and acts upon one type as quickly as upon the other.

Here then is the reason why most people are in the classification of "failures." Most of their thoughts are of failure, and the subconscious mind carries them out to their logical conclusion.

Since the subconscious translates into their logical conclusion all thoughts which reach it—whether they are good or bad for the individual—it is clearly suggested that the way to put the subconscious mind to work for one in a helpful way *is by giving it definite orders as to what is desired.*

When it comes to giving orders to the subconscious mind, there are some instructions which must be carried out to the letter:

(a) Write out a clear statement of that which you wish your subconscious mind to act upon, and set a definite time within which you wish action. Memorize this statement and repeat it to yourself, orally, hundreds of times daily, *especially just before going to sleep.*

(b) When you repeat your statement BELIEVE that it will be acted upon by your subconscious mind, *and see yourself already in possession of that which your statement calls for.* Close your statement by *expressing gratitude* for having received what you asked for.

(c) Before repeating your statement to your subconscious, work yourself into a high, intense state of emotional enthusiasm and joy because of your inner feeling that your request will be fulfilled. The subconscious acts almost instantaneously on thoughts which are *expressed in any state of high emotion*, either negative or positive. This last statement is highly significant. Please read it again and think about it.

HOW TO CONDITION THE MIND FOR DENTISTRY

We come now to the detailed instructions through which one may condition his mind for dentistry, and, by slight changes in the formula, the mind may be conditioned to meet any unpleasant circumstance which one contemplates, such as a major surgical operation, the loss of loved ones in death, etc. The instructions are as follows:

(a) Prepare the entire physical body for the contemplated operation by a three to seven days total fast, which *must* be conducted under the supervision of your physician. Two days prior to the beginning of the fast eat nothing but fresh fruits and drink only fruit juices, also omit *smoking* and *coffee*. You will be somewhat nervous during these two days but do not let that discourage you. At the end of the two days begin your fast and take nothing into your system except water with two or three drops of lemon juice added to each glass. Drink all the water you can—as many as a dozen or more glasses each day.

When the fast ends eat nothing the first day but one

bowl of vegetable soup with no fat in it, and one slice of whole wheat bread, or toast. On the second day eat two bowls of vegetable soup and two slices of bread—one bowl in the forenoon and one in the afternoon. Starting the third day you may eat whatever you please as long as you *eat sparingly*. It is highly important that you come back to your normal eating habits gradually. In general, this is the procedure which should be followed, but every detail of it, including the number of days you should fast, *must be carefully checked by your physician before you begin your fast*.

The purpose of the fast, physically speaking, is to give your entire physical system, your stomach, your digestive organs, your eliminative system, your blood stream, an opportunity to take a vacation. The purpose of the fast, mentally speaking, *is to let you prove to yourself that you are the master of your stomach*. Once you have mastered your desire for food you will have little or no difficulty in mastering your fear of physical pain.

Still another purpose of the fast is that it *conditions your mind for easy communication with your subconscious mind*. During your fast your subconscious mind will be very sensitive to all influences around you, so beware of negative people and the discussion of negative subjects.

(b) Beginning on the first day of your fast, give yourself a treatment, through autosuggestion, by repeating the following instruction to your subconscious mind at least once every hour, except when you are asleep, during your entire fast:
1. I have complete confidence in _____, my dentist, in his skill, his character and his experience in dentistry.
2. While my dental work is being performed by my dentist I shall completely disassociate my mind from it

by keeping my mind on the thing I desire most in life, which is _____

_____

3. I desire my dental work to be done because it will add to my personal appearance and improve my physical health; and because I so desire it, I shall go through the operation as a welcome opportunity to prove to myself that my mind is stronger than the emotion of fear.
4. I hereby direct my subconscious mind to take over my desire, as I have expressed it, and carry it out in every detail, and thus make my dental experience a magnificent interlude. Through this experience I shall make discoveries concerning the powers of my mind *with which I shall guide my entire future so as to get more joy out of life.*

These instructions are simple and understandable, but they will introduce you to a new way of life which may smooth your path in all your future experiences and human relations, as well as carry you through your dental operation without the slightest annoyance.

In these instructions I have introduced you to the most favorable condition under which you may give directives to your subconscious mind—during a fast. Under this condition your subconscious mind will be very alert and amenable to any influence which you may direct to it, or any influence which may get to it by your neglect to keep away from negative influences.

Now let us have a few words concerning the subject of fasting. Here are some of the benefits available through the habit of fasting, quite aside from the fact that fasting is an excellent method of preparing your subconscious mind to receive and carry out your directives:

(a) The habit of fasting, which should be carried on at least once or twice every year, tones up the entire physical body and aids it in building up bodily resistance to disease.

(b) Fasting provides an opportunity whereby one may easily break the habits of smoking and the drinking of coffee and alcoholic beverages. If you smoke or drink alcoholic beverages, as a habit, you will have to learn the habit all over again after you go through your fast, if you wish to smoke or drink again.

(c) Fasting brings one into very close relationship with one's spiritual powers, which is the major reason why directives given to the subconscious mind during a fast are so effective and operate so quickly.

(d) Fasting is an excellent habit for most neurotic and melancholic people who suffer with imaginary ailments, provided always that it is carried on under the supervision of a reputable doctor. Fasting is not child's play, and it never should be undertaken by anyone except by order of a doctor. Doctors in some schools of therapeutics successfully use fasting as a cure for many physical ailments.

(e) Fasting will not be difficult for those who follow the instructions I have here given, and keep their minds busily occupied during the fast, by giving directives to their subconscious minds. This is one of the major reasons for the habit of fasting because it opens wide the gate leading to the subconscious mind, during which any desired instruction may be given to the subconscious.

If you have never gone through a voluntary fast, you have a great treat coming to you when you first experience this practice. You may be slightly nervous the first two days, especially if you drink alcoholic beverages or coffee; but you will have an experience from there on such as you never had before. Recognition that you have mastered your appetite for food will give you a solid foundation on which you can, and perhaps will, develop mastery over many other things, such as poverty and failure and defeat and fear of every type.

Is not this promise worthy of an effort at fasting?

(f) While you are on your fast you will experience the return in memory of things which happened when you were a small child, and you will experience a feeling of self-confidence such as you perhaps never felt previously.

Some years ago, while I was associated with Bernard Macfadden, I had an attack of influenza. After the attack seemed to have passed I had a recurrent spell of it, in a light form, about every two weeks. In speaking of this to Mr. Macfadden he said, "Why don't you go on a fast and starve that flu bug to death? Why keep on feeding it?"

Then he gave me instructions for fasting. I fasted for seven days, under the same instructions I have given here, with the result that the u was completely eliminated, and more important still, I learned from that experience a system of body-conditioning which I have followed ever since—a system which has given me immunity from common colds as well as influenza.

My wife and I go on a fast together, at least annually. We

make a sort of pleasant game out of the habit and get through it without inconvenience or discomfort. Two or more people fasting together, in a pleasant mental attitude, experience even greater benefits than if one were going through the experience alone.

When fasting in preparation for dental or surgical operations, the fasting should be ended at least two weeks before the operations begin. Meanwhile, after the fast is over your doctor should check your system thoroughly and make sure that your blood count, urinal, and heart tests are satisfactory. In some instances, one's diet, after a fasting experience, may need food supplements in the form of vitamins, *but these should be prescribed by your doctor*, not merely purchased on your own judgment. Quite often it happens that following the extraction of teeth, especially where full dentures are indicated, the gums do not heal satisfactorily and the dentist finds it necessary to prescribe food supplements in the form of vitamins.

One other suggestion concerning fasting: Do not engage in any heavy physical activities during the fast. Light housework or office work may be carried on during the fast without interruption, but over-exertions of every nature must be avoided.

There are many good books on the subject of fasting—a list of which is available at all public libraries. One of the best books on this subject I can recommend is *How to Fast*, by Bernard Macfadden.

Mr. Macfadden so thoroughly conditioned his mind for the mastery of physical pain, through fasting some years ago, that he sat in a dentist's chair and had his teeth removed without the aid of any form of anesthetic. While this shows that pain can be mastered by mind control, I personally believe in anesthetics when it comes to a major surgical operation or the extraction of teeth.

The procedure I have here described could be applied as well to the mastery of poverty and the attainment of opulence, or financial prosperity, as to the conditioning of the mind for dental surgery. One would need only to change the statement of purpose to fit whatever objective was desired.

There are no limitations to the power of the mind save only those which the individual establishes for himself, or permits to be established by the influences outside of himself.

Truly, whatever the mind can *conceive* and *believe*, the mind can *achieve!*

Study well the three key words in the foregoing sentence because they epitomize the sum and the substance of this entire chapter.

Your success in the application of the mind-conditioning formula presented in this chapter will depend very largely upon the *mental attitude* in which you apply it. If you BELIEVE you will get satisfactory results, you will get them.

When you give directives to your subconscious mind, through the statement herein which was prepared for that purpose, you may hasten success *by repeating the statement in the form of a prayer*, and thereby place the entire power of your religious BELIEF back of your statement.

The word BELIEF is symbolic of a power that has no limitations within reason and we find evidence of its influence wherever we find people who have achieved noteworthy success in any calling.

Thomas A. Edison BELIEVED he could perfect an incandescent electric lamp, and that belief carried him successfully through the ten thousand failures before he got the answer for which he had been searching.

Marconi BELIEVED the ether could be made to carry the vibrations of sound without the use of wires, and that belief carried him through many failures until he was finally rewarded by triumph, and gave the world its first wireless means of communication.

Columbus BELIEVED he would find land in an uncharted portion of the Atlantic Ocean, and he sailed on and on until he found it, despite the threatened mutiny of his sailors who were not so blessed as he with the capacity for BELIEF.

Madame Schumann-Heink BELIEVED she could become a great opera singer, although her singing teacher had advised her to go back to her sewing machine and be content as a seamstress. Her BELIEF rewarded her with success.

Helen Keller BELIEVED she could learn to talk despite the fact that she lost her use of speech, sight, and hearing, and her BELIEF restored her speech and helped her to become a shining example of encouragement to all people who are tempted to give up in despair because of some physical affliction.

Henry Ford BELIEVED he could build a horseless buggy that would provide rapid transportation at small cost, and despite the far-flung cry of "crackpot" and the skepticism of the world, he belted the earth with the product of his BELIEF, and made himself immensely wealthy.

Madame Marie Curie BELIEVED that radium metal existed and gave herself the task of finding its source, despite the fact that no one had ever seen radium and no one knew where to start looking for it. Her BELIEF finally revealed the source of that precious metal.

When my son was born without ears, and I was told by the doctor who brought him into the world that he would be deaf all his life, I BELIEVED I had the power to influence nature to improvise a system of hearing for him. So I went to work through his subconscious mind and was rewarded when sixty-five percent of his natural hearing capacity was restored.

And when the time came for me to have all of my teeth extracted in preparation for dentures I BELIEVED—*nay, I knew*—I could go through the operation without the slightest discomfort. I KNEW because times without number I had seen the human mind master physical pain and all other unpleasant circumstances which people meet from time to time. I KNEW because I had learned from experience that my own capacity for BELIEF could remove all obstacles which got in my way, and set aside all of my self-imposed limitations.

The most profound truth known to man is the fact that man alone has been given the inexorable privilege of controlling and directing his own mind to whatsoever ends he may choose. All other creatures come into life bound by a pattern of "instinct" which they cannot change, and beyond which they cannot act. This distinguishing prerogative suggests that it is the key to man's control of his earthly destiny, and we know that neglect or failure to make use of this prerogative brings definite punishment in the form of misery, poverty, failure, defeat, illness, despair, and other negative states of mind. *We know also that the acceptance and use of this profound prerogative gives man the key to his own destiny.*

Here then is the supreme of miracles—THE POWER TO TAKE POSSESSION OF ONE'S OWN MIND AND TO DIRECT IT, SUCCESSFULLY, TO WHATEVER ENDS ONE MAY CHOOSE.

And another miracle of only slightly less distinction consists in the fact that along with this profound gift of the right of man to take possession of his own mind, there has been provided the source of power with which to make this gift limitless in man's achievements. This secondary miracle is the subconscious section of the mind through which man may contact and draw upon the universal powers of Infinite Intelligence.

The method by which one may contact Infinite Intelligence through the means of the subconscious mind is simple; it consists in the repetition of a thought, desire, or purpose, by bringing it into the conscious mind often and expressing it orally, in a state of high emotional feeling, thus enabling the subconscious mind to act upon it intelligently. The *SUBCONSCIOUS MIND WILL NOT ACT UPON ANY IDEA, PLAN, OR PURPOSE WHICH IS NOT CLEARLY EXPRESSED TO IT.*

In the preceding sentence you have a clue as to the major reason why so many people fail to get satisfactory results from their subconscious minds. Also you have the major reason why most people are failures instead of successes.

When you give directives to your subconscious mind, be definite and clearly state your desires, and you will not be disappointed, provided you emotionalize your directives with strong BELIEF that they will be carried out. *By this procedure the power which operates the Universe will be at your disposal!*

Points to Remember

1. Stop abusing the power of the human mind and use it purposefully.
2. Your mind is the one thing that you have complete control over.
3. The fear itself is always much worse than the thing which is feared.

2

SPECIALIZED KNOWLEDGE

There are two kinds of knowledge. One is general; the other, specialized. General knowledge, no matter how great in quantity or variety it may be, is of but little use in the accumulation of money. The faculties of the great universities possess, in the aggregate, practically every form of general knowledge known to civilization. *Most of the professors have not amassed great wealth!* They specialize in *teaching* knowledge, but they do not specialize in the organization or the *use* of knowledge for the accumulation of money.

KNOWLEDGE will not attract money (or any other kind of success) unless it is organized and intelligently directed, through practical PLANS OF ACTION, to the DEFINITE END of accumulating money. Lack of understanding of this fact has been the source of confusion to millions of people who falsely believe that "knowledge is power." It is nothing of the sort! Knowledge is only *potential* power. It becomes power only when, and if, it is organized into definite plans of action and directed to a definite end.

This "missing link" in all systems of education known to civilization today may be found in the failure of educational institutions to teach their students HOW TO ORGANIZE AND USE KNOWLEDGE AFTER THEY ACQUIRE IT.

Many people make the mistake of assuming that because Henry Ford had but little schooling, he was not educated. Those who make this mistake did not know Henry Ford, nor do they understand the real meaning of the word "educate." The word is derived from the Latin word *educo*, meaning to educe, to draw out, to DEVELOP FROM WITHIN.

An educated person is not necessarily one who has an abundance of general or specialized knowledge. To be truly educated is to have so developed the faculties of mind that one may acquire anything one wishes, or its equivalent, without violating the rights of others. Henry Ford comes well within the meaning of this definition.

During World War I, a Chicago newspaper published certain editorials in which, among other statements, Henry Ford was called "an ignorant pacifist." Mr. Ford objected to the statements and brought suit against the paper for libeling him. When the suit was tried in the courts, the attorneys for the paper pleaded justification and placed Mr. Ford himself on the witness stand for the purpose of proving to the jury that he was ignorant. The attorneys asked Mr. Ford a great variety of questions, all of them intended to prove by his own evidence that, while he might possess considerable specialized knowledge pertaining to the manufacture of automobiles, he was, in the main, ignorant.

Mr. Ford was plied with such questions as the following: "Who was Benedict Arnold?" and "How many soldiers did the British send over to America to put down the Rebellion of 1776?" In answer to the last question, Mr. Ford replied, "I do not know the exact number of soldiers the British sent over, but I have heard that it was a considerably larger number than ever went back."

Finally, Mr. Ford became tired of this line of questioning,

and in reply to a particularly offensive question, he leaned over, pointed his finger at the lawyer who had asked the question, and said, "If I should really WANT to answer the foolish question you have just asked or any of the other questions you have been asking me, let me remind you that I have a row of electric push-buttons on my desk, and by pushing the right button, I can summon to my aid men who can answer ANY question I desire to ask concerning the business to which I am devoting most of my efforts. Now, will you kindly tell me WHY I should clutter up my mind with general knowledge for the purpose of being able to answer questions when I have men around me who can supply any knowledge I require?"

There certainly was good logic to that reply. The answer floored the lawyer. Every person in the courtroom realized it was the answer not of an ignorant man, but of a man of EDUCATION. Any person is educated who knows where to get knowledge when it is needed and how to organize that knowledge into definite plans of action. Through the assistance of his Master Mind Group, Henry Ford had at his command all the specialized knowledge he needed to enable him to become one of the wealthiest individuals in America. *It was not essential that he have this knowledge in his own mind.* Surely no person who has sufficient inclination and intelligence to read a book of this nature can possibly miss the significance of this illustration.

SPECIALIZED KNOWLEDGE

Before you can be sure of your ability to transmute DESIRE into its monetary equivalent, you will require SPECIALIZED KNOWLEDGE of the service, merchandise, or profession which you intend to offer in return for fortune. Perhaps you may need much more specialized knowledge than you have the ability or the inclination to acquire, and if this should be true, you may bridge your weakness through the aid of your Master Mind Group. Andrew Carnegie stated that he personally knew nothing about the technical end of the steel business. Moreover, he did not particularly care to know anything about it. The specialized knowledge which he required for the manufacture and marketing of steel he found available through the individual units of his MASTER MIND GROUP.

The accumulation of great fortunes calls for POWER, and power is acquired through highly organized and intelligently directed specialized knowledge, but that knowledge does not necessarily have to be in the possession of the person who accumulates the fortune.

The preceding paragraph should give hope and encouragement to the person who has ambition to accumulate a fortune, but who does not have the necessary education to supply such specialized knowledge as may be required. People sometimes go through life suffering from inferiority complexes because they are not "well educated." Yet, the individual who can organize and direct a Master Mind Group of people who possess knowledge useful in the accumulation of money is just as educated as anyone in the group. REMEMBER THAT if you suffer from a feeling of inferiority because your schooling has been limited.

Thomas A. Edison had only three months of formal education during his entire life. Yet he did not lack education, nor did he die poor.

Henry Ford had less than a sixth grade schooling, but he managed to do pretty well by himself financially.

SPECIALIZED KNOWLEDGE is among the most plentiful and the cheapest forms of service which may be had! If you doubt this, consult the payroll of any college or university.

IT PAYS TO KNOW HOW TO PURCHASE KNOWLEDGE

First of all, decide the sort of specialized knowledge you require and the purpose for which it is needed. To a large extent, your major purpose in life, the goal toward which you are working, will help determine what knowledge you need. With this question settled, your next move requires that you have accurate information concerning dependable sources of knowledge. The more important of these are:

(a) your own experience and education
(b) experience and education available through cooperation of others (Master Mind Alliance)
(c) colleges and universities
(d) public libraries (through books and periodicals in which may be found all the knowledge organized by civilization)
(e) special training courses (through night schools and home study materials in particular)

As knowledge is acquired, it must be organized and put into use, for a definite purpose, through practical plans. Knowledge has no value except that which can be gained from its application toward some worthy end. This is one reason why a college degree in itself is not valued more highly. It often represents nothing but miscellaneous knowledge.

If you contemplate pursuing additional formal education, first determine the purpose for which you want the knowledge you are seeking, then learn where this particular sort of knowledge can be obtained from reliable sources.

Successful people, in all callings, never stop acquiring specialized knowledge related to their major purpose, business, or profession. Those who are not successful usually make the mistake of believing that the "knowledge-acquiring" period ends when one finishes school. The truth is that formal education does but little more than to put one in the way of learning how to acquire practical knowledge.

We find ourselves in a Changed World today, and we have also seen some astounding changes in educational requirements. The order of the day is SPECIALIZATION. This truth was emphasized by Robert P. Moore, quoted in a piece written when he was an administrator at Columbia University:

SPECIALISTS MOST SOUGHT

Particularly sought after by employing companies are candidates who have specialized in some field—business school graduates with training in accounting and statistics, engineers of all varieties, journalists, architects, chemists, and also outstanding leaders...of the senior class.

The [graduate] who has been active on the campus, whose personality is such that he or she gets along with all kinds of people and who has done an adequate job with studies has a most decided edge over the strictly academic student. Some of these, because of their all-around qualifications, have received several offers of positions, a few of them as many as six.

In departing from the conception that the 'straight A' student was invariably the one to get the choice of the better jobs, Mr. Moore said that most companies look not only to academic records but to activity records and personalities of the students.

One of the largest industrial companies, the leader in its field, in writing to Mr. Moore concerning prospective seniors at the college, said:

"We are interested primarily in finding people who can

make exceptional progress in management work. For this reason we emphasize qualities of character, intelligence and personality far more than specific educational background."

APPRENTICESHIP PROPOSED

Proposing a system of "apprenticing" students in offices, stores and industrial occupations during the summer vacation, Mr. Moore asserts that after the first two or three years of college, every student should be asked "to choose a definite future course and to call a halt if the student has been merely pleasantly drifting without purpose through an unspecialized academic curriculum.

"Colleges and universities must face the practical consideration that all professions and occupations now demand specialists," he said, urging that educational institutions accept more direct responsibility for vocational guidance.

One of the most reliable and practical sources of knowledge available to those who need specialized training is the night schools operated in most large cities. And correspondence schools give specialized training anywhere the U.S. mails go, on all subjects that can be taught by the extension method. America is also blessed with an abundance of self-study books, courses, and other materials which one may use to acquire specialized training and knowledge. One advantage, in particular, of self-study training is the flexibility of the study program which permits one to study during spare time, during work breaks, or during travel.

Anything acquired without effort and without cost is generally unappreciated, often discredited. Perhaps this is why we get so little from our marvelous opportunity in public schools. The SELF-DISCIPLINE one receives from a definite program of specialized study makes up, to some extent, for the wasted opportunity when knowledge was available without cost.

I learned this from experience early in my career. I enrolled for a home study course in advertising. After completing eight or ten lessons I stopped studying, but the school did not stop sending me bills. Moreover, it insisted upon payment whether I kept up my studies or not. I decided that if I had to pay for the course (which I had legally obligated myself to do), I should complete the lessons and get my money's worth. I felt at the time that the collection system of the school was somewhat too well organized, but I learned later in life that it was a valuable part of my training for which no charge had been made. Being forced to pay, I went ahead and completed the course. Later in life I discovered that the efficient collection system of that school had been worth much to me in the form of money I would later earn because of the training in advertising I had so reluctantly taken.

We have in this country the greatest public school system in the world. We have invested fabulous sums for fine buildings. We have provided convenient transportation for children living in rural and other areas. But there is one astounding weakness to this marvelous system—IT IS FREE! One of the strange things about human beings is that they value only that which has a price. The free schools of America and the free public libraries do not impress people *because they are free* (or appear to be so). This is the major reason why so many people find it necessary to acquire additional training after they quit school and go to work. It is also one of the major reasons why EMPLOYERS GIVE GREATER CONSIDERATION TO EMPLOYEES WHO PARTICIPATE REGULARLY IN SELF-STUDY COURSES AND OTHER FORMS OF PROFESSIONAL DEVELOPMENT. They have learned from experience that any person who has the ambition to give up a part of his or her spare time, or to use slack time at work, for professional development, has those qualities which make for leadership. This recognition is not a charitable gesture. It is sound business judgment upon the part of the employers.

FUEL THAT DRIVE

There is one weakness in people for which there is no remedy. It is the universal weakness of LACK OF AMBITION! People, especially those on salary, who schedule their spare time and slack time to provide for self-improvement seldom remain at the bottom very long. Their action opens the way for the upward climb, removes many obstacles from their path, and gains the friendly interest of those who have the power to put them in the way of OPPORTUNITY.

The self-improvement or "home study" method of training is especially suited to the needs of employed people who find, after leaving school, that they must acquire additional specialized knowledge, but cannot spare the time to go back to school.

The changed economic conditions that now prevail have made it necessary for thousands of people to find additional or new sources of income. For the majority of these, the solution to their problem may be found only by acquiring specialized knowledge. Many will be forced to change their occupation entirely. When merchants find that a certain line of merchandise is not selling, they usually supplant it with another that is in demand. The person whose business is that of marketing personal services must also be an efficient merchant. If the services do not bring adequate returns in one occupation, the individual must change to another, where broader opportunities are available.

Stuart Austin Wier prepared himself as a construction engineer and followed this line of work until the Depression limited his market to where it did not give him the income he required. He took inventory of himself, decided to change his profession to law, went back to school, and took special courses by which he prepared himself as a corporation lawyer. Despite the fact the Depression had not ended, he completed his training, passed the bar examination, and quickly built a lucrative law practice in Dallas, Texas. He actually had to turn away clients.

Just to keep the record straight and to anticipate the alibis of those who will say, "I couldn't go to school because I have a family to support" or "I'm too old," I will add that Mr. Wier was past 40 and married when he went back to school. Moreover, by carefully selecting highly specialized courses, in colleges best prepared to teach the subjects chosen, Mr. Wier completed in two years the work for which the majority of law students require four years. IT PAYS TO KNOW HOW TO PURCHASE KNOWLEDGE!

The person who stops studying merely because he or she has finished school is forever hopelessly doomed to mediocrity, no matter what that person's calling. The way of success is the way of *continuous pursuit of knowledge*.

Points to Remember

1. Knowledge alone will not attract money unless it is systematically directed.
2. You can be ignorant despite completing the highest levels of education.
3. How to overpower your inferiority complexes.

3

ORGANIZED THOUGHT

"Thoughts are things," said a great philosopher, and it is significant that thought is one of the few things an individual may control completely.

Thought "magnetizes" one's entire physical body, and attracts to one the outward, physical things which harmonize. The burden of this chapter is to show how the power of thought can be organized and directed toward definite ends.

This chapter is illustrated with three charts outlining, as simply as possible, the mechanism of the mind, and the sources of thought stimuli which start action in the mind.

Chart Number 1: Here is presented the route that must be taken in organizing thought and expressing it in the attainment of a definite end. Observe that the starting point is desire, based upon one or more of the nine basic motives which inspire action. The stimulus needed to keep desire active is supplied by some combination of the known principles of individual achievement.

Chart Number 2: Here is shown the three steps which must be taken in the attainment of the object of one's Definite Major Purpose, together with the principles which must be combined and applied in the effective use of organized thought.

Chart Number 3: Here is shown the ten factors which constitute the "mechanism" of thought, showing the sources of stimuli of thought. Observe that the subconscious mind is connected with all departments of the mind, and its source of power is Infinite Intelligence. Observe, also, that the memory, the five senses, and the emotions require constant self-discipline; that they are not reliable without the strictest of discipline; and that they need highly organized attention to bring them under control. This control is obtained by the exercise of the power of will, through the adoption of voluntary habits.

CHART NUMBER 1

DESIRE
THE STARTING
POINT OF ALL
ACHIEVEMENT
BASED ON
A COMBINATION
OF

ATTAINED THROUGH
SOME COMBINATION OF
THE SEVENTEEN PRINCIPLES
OF ACHIEVEMENT

1. Definiteness of purpose
2. The Master Mind Alliance
3. Attractive Personality
4. Applied Faith
5. Going the Extra Mile
6. Organized Endeavor
7. Applied Golden Rule
8. Inspired Feeling
9. Self-discipline
10. Organized thought
11. Controlled Attention
12. Team Work
13. Liberty of thought
14. Learning from defeat
15. Creative Vision
16. Health maintenance
17. Budgeting time and money

THE NINE BASIC MOTIVES

1. Emotion of LOVE
2. Emotion of SEX
3. Desire for HEALTH
4. Desire for SELF-PRESERVATION
5. Desire for FREEDOM OF BODY AND MIND
6. Desire for PERSONAL EXPRESSION AND FAME
7. Desire for PERPETUATION OF LIFE
8. Desire for REVENGE
9. Emotion of FEAR: based on seven basics fears: Fear of Poverty, Criticism, Ill Health, Loss of Love, Old Age, Loss of Liberty, Death.

MAJOR
PURPOSE
IN LIFE
*FINISHING
POINT*

CHART NUMBER 2

This Chart Shows the Order in Which Organized Thought Should Be Applied in the Attainment of Any Desired Purpose

DEFINITE MAJOR PURPOSE (First Step)

Can be attained through the factors listed below, in the order here shown. Proceeding according to this chart is, of itself, an effective form of Organized Thought.

Don't forget that your purpose should be founded on a definite motive, or some combination of the nine basic motives:

PLAN OF ATTAINMENT (Second Step)

Success can be no greater than the plan is sound; therefore enlist help in building plans.

MASTERMIND ALLIANCE (Third Step)

Choose your "Master Mind" allies so as to procure experience and knowledge needed in carrying out your plan.

THE FOLLOWING PRINCIPLES ARE NECESSARY IN PROCEEDING UNDER ORGANIZED THOUGHT

1. Organized Thought
2. Applied Faith
3. Organized Endeavor
4. Creative Vision
5. Self-discipline
6. Going the Extra Mile
7. Attractive Personality

Study carefully the three important steps one must take, based on (1) definiteness of purpose (2) a sound plan, and (3) a Master Mind alliance with experienced helpers.

CHART NUMBER 3

Chart of the Ten Factors Which Constitute the "Mechanism" of Thought. Observe That the Subconscious Section of the Mind Has Access to All Departments of the Mind, but Is Not Under the Control of Any.

INFINITE INTELLIGENCE

The source of all power of thought, all facts, all knowledge, available through the subconscious section of the mind only.

SUBCONSCIOUS SECTION OF THE MIND
The connecting link between the mind of man and Infinite Intelligence.

Below are shown all departments of the mind, with the three sources of thought stimuli at bottom of the chart.

FACULTY OF WILLPOWER
"Boss of the mind"

FACULTY OF REASON
Master of all opinions and judgments

FACULTY OF EMOTIONS
The seat of most actions of the mind

FACULTY OF IMAGINATION
The builder of all plans

FACULTY OF CONSCIENCE
Moral guide of the mind

The three sources of thought which require the greatest amount of self-discipline are shown below.

INTUITION	THE FIVE SENSES		MEMORY
The "sixth sense" or intuitive knowledge.	1. Sight 2. Sound 3. Taste 4. Smell 5. Touch	These become reliable only through strict self-discipline.	Store house of all thought and sense impressions. Filing cabinet of the brain.

KEY TO CHART NUMBER 3

1. **Infinite Intelligence:** The source of all power of thought, available through the subconscious mind only. Note that the chart shows all departments of the mind entirely encircled by Infinite Intelligence.

2. **Subconscious Mind:** The connecting link between the conscious mind and Infinite Intelligence. Not subject to self-discipline, but can be stimulated by the means described in this chapter.
3. **Faculty of Willpower:** "Boss" of all departments of the mind, with the power to modify, change, or "balance" the actions of all mental functions.
4. **Faculty of Reason:** "Presiding judge" that may, if it is permitted, pass judgment on all ideas, plans, and desires; but its decisions can be set aside by the power of will, or offset by the influence of the emotions when the will does not assert itself.
5. **Faculty of Emotions:** The seat of most of the actions of the mind, the source of most of the thoughts released by the mind, and may be very dangerous if not modified by the faculty of reason, under the direction of the power of will.
6. **Faculty of Imagination:** The builder of all plans, ideas, and ways and means of attaining desired ends. Needs self-discipline and constant direction of the power of will to avoid exaggeration.
7. **Faculty of Conscience:** Moral guide of the mind whose chief function is that of modifying the individual's aims and purposes so they harmonize with moral laws.
8. **Intuition:** The "sixth sense" by which one makes decisions based on subconscious information.
9. **The Five Senses:** The physical "arms" of the brain through which it contacts the external world and acquires information. The senses are not reliable, and need constant discipline. Under any form of highly emotional activity the senses become confused and highly undependable, as in the case of fear.
10. **Memory:** The "filing cabinet" of the brain, wherein is stored

all thought impulses, all experiences, and all sensations that reach the brain through the five physical senses. Also undependable, and needs self-discipline for perfection.

SOME OF THE KNOWN FACTS CONCERNING THE NATURE OF THOUGHT

1. All thought (whether positive or negative, good or bad, accurate or inaccurate) tends to clothe itself in its physical equivalent, and it proceeds by inspiring one with ideas, plans, and means of attaining desired ends, through perfectly logical and natural media. After thought on a given subject becomes a habit, it is taken over by the subconscious mind and automatically acted upon, through the most available media. Everything is the tool of thought! It may not be literally true that "thoughts are things," but it is true that thoughts create things, and the things they create are striking duplicates of the thoughts out of which they are fashioned.
2. Through the application of self-discipline thought can be influenced, controlled, and directed through transmutation toward a desired end, by the development of voluntary habits suitable for the attainment of any given end.
3. The power of thought (with the aid of the subconscious mind) has control over every cell of the body, encourages the cells in repair, stimulates their growth, influences all the organs of the body, helps them to function orderly, and assists in fighting disease through what is commonly called "body resistance." These functions are carried on automatically, but they may be stimulated by voluntary aid.
4. All of man's achievements begin in the form of thought, organized into plans, aims, and purposes, and expressed in

terms of action. All action is stimulated by one or more of the nine basic motives, as shown in Chart Number 1.

5. There are two sections of the mind that deal with thought, the conscious and the subconscious. The conscious section, operating through the five departments of the mind, is under the control of man. The subconscious section is under the control of Infinite Intelligence. (See Chart Number 3.) The "sixth sense" is under the control of the subconscious section of the mind, and it functions automatically.

6. Both the subconscious and the conscious sections of the mind work in response to habits, adjusting themselves to whatever habits the individual may form, whether the habits are voluntary or involuntary. When habits are once formed, the mind proceeds to carry them out automatically, unless they are modified by other and stronger habits.

7. The majority of all thoughts acted upon by the mind are not necessarily accurate, being based on personal "opinions," bias, prejudice, fear, and the result of emotional excitement in which the faculty of reason has been given little opportunity to modify them rationally. The five senses are so untrustworthy that they can be easily deceived, especially when they function under emotional excitement, such as fear, love, sex, or in fact any of the other emotions, without the "balancing" influence of the faculty of reason.

8. The first step in accurate thinking is that of separating facts from mere indications or hearsay evidence.

9. The second step is that of separating facts (after they have been identified as such) into two classes, viz.: important and unimportant. An important fact is any fact which can be used to help one attain the object of one's major purpose. All other facts are relatively unimportant. The average

person spends his life dealing with "inferences" based upon unreliable sources of information, and seldom comes within sight of that form of self-discipline which demands facts. Moreover, the average person never, during his entire lifetime, learns to distinguish the difference between "important" and "unimportant" facts, which may account for there being so many failures in the world. It is a matter of evaluation—putting first things first.

10. Desire, based on a definite motive, is the beginning of all voluntary thought action associated with individual achievement. The presence in the mind of an intense desire tends to stimulate the faculty of imagination with the purpose of creating ways and means of attaining the object of the desire. If the desire is persistently held in the mind through repetition of thought it is picked up by the subconscious section of the mind and automatically carried out to its logical conclusion, by the most practical means available.

11. The known sources of stimulation of thought are:
    a. The five physical senses (very unreliable).
    b. The storehouse of the memory (also unreliable).
    c. The subconscious mind, through which thought may be stimulated by the influence of Infinite Intelligence. It is believed by many that this is the source of thought stimulation of those who are recognized as "geniuses," the assumption being that the person who, through self-discipline and practice, develops the ability to use his subconscious mind at will thereby places himself in a position to draw upon the power of Infinite Intelligence for guidance in carrying out his aims and purposes.
    d. The emotions, the seat of all desires. From this source comes all the thought stimulation based upon the

major emotions, and inasmuch as these emotional feelings express themselves voluntarily it is necessary to gain control over them, through self-discipline. This is the source from which most of the thought stimulation arises, a fact which accounts for the saying that "emotion rules the world."

e. Faculty of the will, the "boss" of all other departments of the mind. Although this faculty is the "boss" of the mind, it has been mentioned last for the reason that it is used the least, by the majority of people. By far the greater part of all thought stimulation of the average person comes from the emotions, and neither the faculty of reason nor the willpower is consulted in connection with most of these thoughts, an error which is responsible for so many mistakes in judgment of which the majority of people are guilty.

As far as is known, these five sources are the only sources of thought stimulation. Study them carefully (in Chart Number 3) and establish a clear picture in your mind of the factors you must deal with in order to acquire the ability to organize your thoughts. This chart should be consulted regularly until you understand it, for it is an actual "picture" of the working equipment of all thinking. The chart cannot be mastered by a casual glance.

UNCOVERING THE MECHANISMS BEHIND BRAIN OPERATIONS

Begin your study of the chart by observing that Infinite Intelligence, the source of all power of thought, is placed at the top. Observe, also, that no faculty of the mind has direct connection with Infinite Intelligence; but all departments of the mind have access to it through the medium of the subconscious section of the mind.

You will notice that the first five departments of the mind (willpower, reason, emotions, imagination, and conscience) are connected separately with the subconscious section of the mind; also, they are connected directly with one another.

The three sources of thought stimulation at the bottom of the chart (intuition, the five senses, and memory) have been separated from the other departments of the mind for the reason that they are the three sources of thought stimulation which are the least subject to the control of the will; therefore they need special attention through strict self-discipline.

Three faculties of the mind (reason, imagination, and conscience) perform definite functions in the process of thinking but apparently no thought stimulation comes from these. All three of these faculties modify thought after it is submitted to them but they do not originate thought. The faculty of reason compares all thought with one's past experience (as recalled from the memory) and forms all judgments and opinions. The faculty of the imagination shapes one's thoughts into ideas, plans, and ways and means of attaining desired ends. The conscience gives moral guidance to all thoughts. If consulted at all times, before one engages in expressing any thought in terms of action, these three faculties of the mind will become strong and dependable. If they are not consulted, and one forms the habit of acting on thought without their modifying influence, they will atrophy and become useless.

All faculties of the mind may be developed and made dependable in the same manner that one may develop a strong arm, namely, by systematic use, through organized habits of thought. There is no other way to gain control over the mind except systematic use, under a plan that will give recognition to every department of the mind, according to the instructions outlined here.

Do not become discouraged if you do not grasp the complete plan of the operation of the mind the first time you read this chapter.

It is no easy matter to draw a picture of the operation of the mind so it can be understood at a glance. Read the chapter through; then lay it aside and do some thinking on your own account, coming back to the three charts to refresh your memory from time to time. If you master this chapter after a dozen such readings, you will be fortunate. Remember, however, that all the time you spend will be justified because you are here dealing with the most important force that affects your life—the subject of accurate thinking.

BELIEVE, THEN SUCCEED

Let me here introduce another factor of great importance in organized thinking—one that has not been included in any charts. It is the importance of acquiring the necessary self-discipline to enable you to believe. For example, when you adopt a Definite Major Purpose you must focus all your emotional feeling on the object of that purpose, in a spirit of absolute belief in its attainment.

Let your daily slogan be, "You can do it if you believe you can!"

By some strange power with which no one is familiar, the subconscious mind acts directly and immediately upon the thoughts which are based upon absolute belief, and proceeds to carry such thoughts out to their logical conclusion by practical and natural media which are available.

All great leaders are able believers! There are certain basic requirements of success in which one must believe in order to succeed. Some of them are:

a. Belief in Infinite Intelligence (God).
b. Belief in one's self.
c. Belief in one's chosen associates.
d. Belief in right over wrong; that right will prevail if one persists in believing in right.
e. Belief in the proven laws and facts of science.
f. Belief in the power of the mind to connect itself with Infinite Intelligence and become, therefore, irresistible.

Belief in these six subjects is a fundamental requirement of success. Accept them as such, and do not stop until you automatically believe in them all.

As strange as it may seem, the greatest power available to mankind is an intangible power, neither the nature nor the source of which is understood. It is man's only irresistible power, and there is but one way in which it can be appropriated and used in the practical affairs of daily life.

This power has given the world the best of everything that we enjoy in modern life. It has made the United States the richest and the freest country in the world. It has won every war in which this country has engaged. It has built the great system of railroads and the powerful industrial empire of America. It has uncovered a myriad of useful inventions. It has conquered the air and mastered the oceans. It has given us the power of instantaneous communication with nearly all parts of the earth. It has given us the highest standard of living known to civilization.

Stated in one sentence, it is "the capacity of men to believe in something." Just that alone, without any modifying definitions; the simple, clearly demonstrable power of belief; the power that has worked miracles down through the ages. Not all the scientific knowledge known to mankind can cope with this intangible form of power. It baffles the minds of the shrewdest of men and defies analysis. It has nothing in common with logic or reason, and it overrides both at will. It is a law unto itself, and the strangest feature of this power is that it can be appropriated and used by the humblest person the same as by the most educated and renowned.

George Washington believed his little handful of soldiers could whip a vastly superior army and then they did it, although his achievement has remained one of the most baffling military triumphs of all times.

Edison believed that he could harness electric energy and make it serve as a light. He stood steadfastly behind that belief through more than ten thousand failures and lived to see his belief justified, although others before him had tried to accomplish the same result and failed—failed, perhaps, because they lacked the capacity for unshakable belief.

James J. Hill believed that he could bring the East and the West together with a great transcontinental railroad, and though he was only a humble telegraph operator, without money and with few influential friends, he translated his belief into a splendid reality.

The Wright brothers believed they could build a machine that would carry a man safely through the air and backed that belief persistently through many heartbreaking failures until, at long last, they proved once more that even the law of gravitation is no match for the power of man's belief.

Search the records of mankind wherever you will, go as far back as you please, and you will discover that the strong men, the great men, the successful men, have been those who believed in something.

The world belongs to men who believe! It always has and it always will. Therefore, in organizing your mind power be sure to include in your plans a definite program of belief in the things you wish to become real. Let your belief be positive. Believe in something, not against something, remembering meanwhile that belief is contagious; that belief in one thing tends to open the way for belief in many things, while unbelief works in the same manner.

No one can rise above mediocrity unless he believes in his own ability to become and to remain self-determining. A student of this philosophy who had just discovered how to take possession of his own mind, through organization of his mind power, expressed his gratitude for the new power revealed to him in these words:

> I thank God for unwinding
> The tangled skein of my life,
> Thereby freeing my mind forever
> From all forms of fear and strife.

Truly, the mind that has been brought under self-discipline, through proper organization of the departments of the mind, may be "forever free from all forms of fear and strife." A disorganized mind can never be free. Mind organization must begin with an inventory of the factors which enter into thinking, as they have been presented in Chart Number 3. These factors must be brought under self-discipline and directed to definite ends, through Organized Endeavor. The mind develops and becomes strong only through action. Even belief is useless unless it is followed by some sort of action appropriate to its nature and purpose. Passive belief produces no results whatsoever save failure and defeat.

And this is a privilege which the Creator left to every human being! To emphasize the great possibilities of this privilege it was singled out and made the only privilege over which any human being has complete control. Men may lose all their worldly possessions, including sound health. They may be cheated, imposed upon, maligned, and slandered by others, or they may be unjustly thrown into prison and deprived of their physical liberty, but they still may think their own thoughts and use their own mind power without the consent of any other person.

How inconsistent it is that the only thing over which a human being has complete control is the one thing which most people make the least attempt to control. The inconsistency becomes all the more astounding when one recognizes the fact that the power of organized thought offers the solution to all of one's problems, and nothing else does.

Test this statement by any circumstance of life you choose and observe how accurate it is. Whatever man desires, he may acquire with the aid of his power of thought, provided he will organize his thoughts and apply his thought power in a spirit of belief in his own ability to make it serve his needs. Thought, applied in a spirit of belief, unlocks prison doors and gives men their freedom. It develops body resistance and frees men from disease where everything else fails. It supplants poverty with opulence. It dispels fear, worry, and discouragement and fills their places with hope, faith, and peace of mind. Moreover, it works with the speed of lightning, requiring nothing but a determined will to put it into action.

Points to Remember

1. Organize and direct your power of thoughts towards definite ends.
2. Willpower is the "boss" of all compartments of the mind.
3. Learn to distinguish between important and unimportant thoughts.

4

A DEFINITE CHIEF AIM

Singleness of purpose is essential for success, no matter what may be one's idea of the definition of success. Yet singleness of purpose is a quality which may, and generally does, call for thought on many allied subjects.

A well organized, alert and energetic mind is produced by various and sundry stimuli, all of which are plainly described in these lessons.

It should be remembered, however, that the mind requires, for its development, a variety of exercise, just as the physical body, to be properly developed, calls for many forms of systematic exercise.

Horses are trained to certain gaits by trainers who hurdle-jump them over handicaps which cause them to develop the desired steps, through habit and repetition. The human mind must be trained in a similar manner, by a variety of thought-inspiring stimuli.

You will observe, before you have gone very far into this philosophy, that the reading of these lessons will super induce a flow of thoughts covering a wide range of subjects. For this reason the student should read the course with a notebook and pencil at hand, and follow the practice of recording these thoughts or "ideas" as they come into the mind.

By following this suggestion the student will have a collection of ideas, by the time the course has been read two or three times, sufficient to transform his or her entire life-plan.

By following this practice it will be noticed, very soon, that the mind has become like a magnet in that it will attract useful ideas right out of the "thin air," to use the words of a noted scientist who has experimented with this principle for a great number of years.

You will do yourself a great injustice if you undertake this course with even a remote feeling that you do not stand in need of more knowledge than you now possess. In truth, no man knows enough about any worthwhile subject to entitle him to feel that he has the last word on that subject.

In the long, hard task of trying to wipe out some of my own ignorance and make way for some of the useful truths of life, I have often seen, in my imagination, the Great Marker who stands at the gateway entrance of life and writes "Poor Fool" on the brow of those who believe they are wise, and "Poor Sinner" on the brow of those who believe they are saints.

Which, translated into workaday language, means that none of us know very much, and by the very nature of our being can never know as much as we need to know in order to live sanely and enjoy life while we live.

Humility is a forerunner of success!

Until we become humble in our own hearts we are not apt to profit greatly by the experiences and thoughts of others.

Sounds like a preachment on morality? Well, what if it does?

Even "preachments," as dry and lacking in interest as they generally are, may be beneficial if they serve to reflect the shadow of our real selves so we may get an approximate idea of our smallness and superficiality.

Success in life is largely predicated upon our knowing men!

The best place to study the man-animal is in your own mind, by taking as accurate an inventory as possible of YOURSELF. When you know yourself thoroughly (if you ever do) you will also know much about others.

To know others, not as they seem to be, but as they really are, study them through:

1. The posture of the body, and the way they walk.
2. The tone of the voice, its quality, pitch, volume.
3. The eyes, whether shifty or direct.
4. The use of words, their trend, nature and quality.

This philosophy is intended to enable those who master it to "sell" their way through life successfully, with the minimum amount of resistance and friction. Such a course, therefore, must help the student organize and make use of much truth which is overlooked by the majority of people who go through life as mediocres.

Not all people are so constituted that they wish to know the truth about all matters vitally affecting life. One of the great surprises the author of this course has met with, in connection with his research activities, is that so few people are willing to hear the truth when it shows up their own weaknesses.

We prefer illusions to realities!

New truths, if accepted at all, are taken with the proverbial grain of salt. Some of us demand more than a mere pinch of salt; we demand enough to pickle new ideas so they become useless.

For these reasons the Introductory Lesson of this course, and this lesson as well, cover subjects intended to pave the way for new ideas so those ideas will not be too severe a shock to the mind of the student.

RISKS ASSOCIATED WITH NEW IDEAS

The thought the author wishes to "get across" has been quite plainly stated by the editor of the American Magazine, in an editorial which appeared in a recent issue, in the following words:

> On a recent rainy night, Carl Lomen, the reindeer king of Alaska, told me a true story. It has stuck in my crop ever since. And now I am going to pass it along.
>
> "A certain Greenland Eskimo," said Lomen, "was taken on one of the American North Polar expeditions a number of years ago. Later, as a reward for faithful service, he was brought to New York City for a short visit. At all the miracles of sight and sound he was filled with a most amazed wonder. When he returned to his native village he told stories of buildings that rose into the very face of the sky; of street cars, which he described as houses that moved along the trail, with people living in them as they moved; of mammoth bridges, artificial lights, and all the other dazzling concomitants of the metropolis.
>
> "His people looked at him coldly and walked away. And forthwith throughout the whole village he was dubbed 'Sagdluk,' meaning 'the Liar,' and this name he carried in shame to his grave. Long before his death his original name was entirely forgotten.
>
> "When Knud Rasmussen made his trip from Greenland to Alaska he was accompanied by a Greenland Eskimo named Mitek (Eider Duck). Mitek visited Copenhagen and New York, where he saw many things for the first time and was greatly impressed. Later, upon his return to Greenland, he recalled the tragedy of Sagdluk,

and decided that it would not be wise to tell the truth. Instead, he would narrate stories that his people could grasp, and thus save his reputation.

"So he told them how he and Doctor Rasmussen maintained a kayak on the banks of a great river, the Hudson, and how, each morning, they paddled out for their hunting. Ducks, geese and seals were to be had a-plenty, and they enjoyed the visit immensely.

"Mitek, in the eyes of his countrymen, is a very honest man. His neighbors treat him with rare respect."

The road of the truth-teller has always been rocky. Socrates sipping the hemlock, Christ crucified, Stephen stoned, Bruno burned at the stake, Galileo terrified into retraction of his starry truths—forever could one follow that bloodly trail through the pages of history.

Something in human nature makes us resent the impact of new ideas.

We hate to be disturbed in the beliefs and prejudices that have been handed down with the family furniture. At maturity too many of us go into hibernation, and live off the fat of ancient fetishes. If a new idea invades our den, we rise up snarling from our winter sleep.

The Eskimos, at least, had some excuse. They were unable to visualize the startling pictures drawn by Sagdluk. Their simple lives had been too long circumscribed by the brooding arctic night.

But there is no adequate reason why the average man should ever close his mind to fresh "slants" on life. He does, just the same. Nothing is more tragic—or more common—than mental inertia. For every ten men who are physically lazy there are ten thousand with stagnant minds. And stagnant minds are the breeding places of fear.

An old farmer up in Vermont always used to wind up his prayers with this plea: "Oh, God, give me an open mind!" If more people followed his example they might escape being hamstrung by prejudices. And what a pleasant place to live in the world would be.

◆

Every person should make it his business to gather new ideas from sources other than the environment in which he daily lives and works.

The mind becomes withered, stagnant, narrow and closed unless it searches for new ideas. The farmer should come to the city quite often, and walk among the strange faces and the tall buildings. He will go back to his farm, his mind refreshed, with more courage and greater enthusiasm.

The city man should take a trip to the country every so often and freshen his mind with sights new and different from those associated with his daily labors.

Everyone needs a change of mental environment at regular periods, the same as a change and variety of food are essential. The mind becomes more alert, more elastic and more ready to work with speed and accuracy after it has been bathed in new ideas, outside of one's own field of daily labor.

As a student of this course you will temporarily lay aside the set of ideas with which you perform your daily labors, and enter a field of entirely new (and in some instances, heretofore unheard-of) ideas.

Splendid! You will come out, at the other end of this course, with a new stock of ideas which will make you more efficient, more enthusiastic and more courageous, *no matter in what sort of work you may be engaged.*

Do not be afraid of new ideas! They may mean to you the difference between success and failure.

Points to Remember

1. Singleness of purpose is essential for success.
2. Exercise your mind just as you do for your physical body.
3. Until we become humble in our own hearts we are not apt to profit greatly.

5

INITIATIVE AND LEADERSHIP

Initiative and Leadership are associated terms in this lesson for the reason that *leadership* is essential for the attainment of *Success,* and *Initiative* is the very foundation upon which this necessary quality of *leadership* is built. *Initiative* is as essential to success as a hub is essential to a wagon wheel.

And what is *Initiative?*

It is that exceedingly rare quality that prompts—nay, impels—a person to do that which ought to be done *without being told to do it.* Elbert Hubbard expressed himself on the subject of *initiative* in the words:

"The world bestows its big prizes, both in money and honors, for one thing, and that is *Initiative.*

"What is initiative? I'll tell you: It is doing the right thing without being told.

"But next to doing the right thing without being told is to do it when you are told once. That is say, 'Carry the message to Garcia.' Those who can carry a message get high honors, but their pay is not always in proportion.

"Next, there are those who do the right thing when necessity kicks them from behind, and these 'get indifference instead of honors, and a pittance for pay.

"This kind spend most of the time polishing a bench with

a hard luck story.

"Then, still lower down in the scale than this we have the fellow who will not do the right thing even when someone goes along to show him how and stays to see that he does it; he is always out of a job, a receives the contempt he deserves, unless he has a rich pa, in which case destiny patiently waits around the comer with a stuffed club.

"To which class do *you* belong?"

Inasmuch as you will be expected to take inventory of yourself and determine which factors of this course you need most, after you have completed it, it may be well if you begin to get ready for this analysis by answering the question that Elbert Hubbard has asked:

To which class do you belong?

One of the peculiarities of L*eadership* is the fact that it is never found in those who have not acquired the *habit* of taking the initiative. *Leadership* is something that you must invite yourself into; it will never thrust itself upon you. If you will carefully analyze all leaders whom you know you will see that they not only exercised *Initiative*, but they went about their work with a *definite purpose* in mind.

These facts are mentioned in this lesson for the reason that it will profit you to observe that successful people make use of all the factors covered by the sixteen lessons of the course; and, for the more important reason that it will profit you to understand thoroughly the principle of *organized effort* which this Reading Course is intended to establish in your mind.

This seems an appropriate place to state that this course is not intended as a *shortcut* to success, nor is it intended as a mechanical formula that you may use in noteworthy achievement without effort on your part. The *real* value of the course lies in the *use* that you will make of it, and not in the course itself. The chief purpose of the course is to help you develop in yourself the fifteen qualities covered by the sixteen lessons of the course, and one of the most important of these qualities is *Initiative*, the subject of this lesson.

We will now proceed to apply the principle upon which this lesson is founded by describing, in detail, just how it served successfully to complete a business transaction which most people would call difficult.

In 1916 I needed $25,000.00 with which to create an educational institution, but I had neither this sum nor sufficient collateral with which to borrow it through the usual banking sources. Did I bemoan my fate or think of what I might accomplish if some rich relative or Good Samaritan would come to my rescue by loaning me the necessary capital?

I did nothing of the sort!

I did just what you will be advised, throughout this course, to do. First of all, I made the securing of this capital my *definite chief aim*. Second, I laid out a complete *plan* through which to transform this aim into reality. Backed by sufficient Self-confidence and spurred on by *Initiative*, I proceeded to put my plan into action. But, before the "action" stage of the plan had been reached, more than six weeks of constant, persistent study and effort and thought were embodied in it. If a plan is to be sound it must be built of carefully chosen material.

HOW TO BE AN INITIATOR

There are generally many plans through the operation of which a desired object may be achieved, and it often happens to be true that the obvious and usual methods employed are not the best. The usual method of procedure, in the case related, would have been that of borrowing from a bank. You can see that this method was impractical, in this case, for the reason that no collateral was available.

A great philosopher once said: *"Initiative is the pass-key that opens the door to opportunity "*

I do not recall who this philosopher was, but I know that he was *great* because of the soundness of his statement.

We will now proceed to outline the exact procedure that you must follow if you are to become a person of *initiative* and *leadership*.

First: You must master the habit of *procrastination* and eliminate it from your make-up. This habit of putting off until tomorrow that which you should have done last week or last year or a score of years ago is gnawing at the very vitals of your being, and you can accomplish nothing until you throw it off.

The method through which you eliminate *procrastination* is based upon a well known and scientifically tested principle of psychology which has been referred to in the two preceding lessons of this course as Autosuggestion.

Copy the following formula and place it conspicuously in your room where you will see it as you retire at night and as you arise in the morning:

INITIATIVE AND LEADERSHIP

I realize that the place to begin developing the *habit of initiative* is in the small, commonplace things connected with my daily work, therefore I will go at my work each day as if I were doing it solely for the purpose of developing this necessary *habit of initiative.*

I understand that by practicing this *habit of* taking the *initiative* in connection with my daily work I will be not only developing that habit, but I will also be attracting the attention of those who will place greater value on my services as a result of this practice.

Signed ....

Regardless of what you are now doing, every day brings you face to face with a chance to render some service, outside of the course of your regular duties, that will be of value to others. In rendering this additional service, of your own accord, you of course understand that you are not doing so with the object of receiving monetary pay. You are rendering this service because it provides you with ways and means of exercising, developing and making stronger the aggressive spirit of *initiative* which you must possess before you can ever become an outstanding figure in the affairs of your chosen field of life-work.

Those who work for *money* alone, and who receive for their pay nothing but money, are always underpaid, no matter how much they receive. Money is necessary, but the big prizes of life cannot be measured in dollars and cents.

No amount of money could possibly be made to take the place of the happiness and joy and pride that belong to the person who digs a better ditch, or builds a better chicken coop, or sweeps a cleaner floor, or cooks a better meal. Every normal person loves to create something that is better than the average. The joy of *creating* a work of art is a joy that cannot be replaced by money or any other form of material possession.

The brand of *leadership* that is recommended through this course of instruction is the brand which leads to self-determination and freedom and self-development and enlightenment and justice. This is the brand that endures. For example, and as a contrast with the brand of *leadership* through which Napoleon raised himself into prominence, consider our own American commoner, Lincoln. The object of his *leadership* was to bring truth and justice and understanding to the people of the United States. Even though he died a martyr to his belief in this brand of *leadership*, his name has been engraved upon the heart of the world in terms of loving kindliness that will never bring aught but good to the world.

Points to Remember

1. No one could become an efficient leader without belief in himself.
2. *Initiative* is the very foundation upon which this necessary quality of *leadership* is built.
3. Money is necessary, but the big prizes of life cannot be measured in dollars and cents.

6

GO THE EXTRA MILE

Going the extra mile means rendering of more service and better service than you're paid to render, doing it all the time, and doing it with a pleasant, pleasing mental attitude.

One of the reasons why there are so many failures in the world is that the majority of people do not even go the first mile, let along the second one. If they do go the first mile, they usually gripe as they go along and make themselves a darned nuisance to people around them. I suppose you know the type. But it doesn't apply to any of you, because if you were like that before you got into this philosophy, you're going to get over it very fast.

I don't know of any one quality or trait that can get a person an opportunity quicker than to go out of his or her way to do somebody a favor, or do something useful. It's the one thing you can do in life without having to ask anybody for the privilege of doing it. Unless you form the habit of going the extra mile and make yourself as indispensable as you possibly can, the only other way you'll ever be free, and independent, and self-determining, and financially independent in old age will be by a stroke of good luck, a rich uncle or rich aunt dying, or something of that sort. I don't know of any way anybody can make himself or herself indispensable *except* by going the extra mile, by rendering some sort of service that you're not expected to render, and rendering it in the right sort of a mental attitude.

Mental attitude is important. If you gripe about going the extra mile, chances are that it won't bring you very many returns. Where do you suppose I get my authority for emphasizing this principle of going the extra mile? Experience.

I've watched the way nature does things, because you won't go wrong if you follow the way or the habits of nature. Conversely, if you fail to recognize and follow the way nature does things, you'll get into trouble sooner or later—it's just a question of time. There is an overall plan in which this universe operates, no matter what you call the first cause of that plan, or the operator of it, or the creator of it. There's just one set of natural laws, and it's up to every individual to discover them and adjust himself favorably to them. Above all, nature requests and demands that every living thing go the extra mile in order to eat, in order to live, and in order to survive. Man wouldn't survive one season if it were not for this law of going the extra mile.

Don't render a million dollars' worth of service today and expect to get a bank check for it tomorrow. If you start out to render a million dollars' worth of service, you might have to render it a little bit at a time. You're going to have to get yourself recognized for doing it and you'll have to go the extra mile for a little while before anybody takes notice of you. However, be careful not to go the extra mile *too* long without somebody taking notice of you. If the right fellow doesn't take notice, look around until you find the right fellow who will. In other words, if your present employer doesn't recognize you, fire the employer sooner or later and let his competitor know what kind of service you're rendering. I assure you it won't hurt your chances a bit. Have a little competition as you go along.

Nobody ever accepts a rule or does anything without a motive, and I have a great variety of reasons why you should go the extra mile.

THE LAW OF INCREASING RETURNS

The law of increasing returns means that you'll get back more than you give out, whether it's good or bad, whether it's positive or negative. That's the way the law of nature works. Whatever you give out, whatever you do to or for another person, or whatever you give out from yourself, comes back to you greatly multiplied in kind. No exception whatsoever. It doesn't always come back very quickly; sometimes it takes longer than you expect. But you may be sure that if you send out some negative influence, it's going to come back to you sooner or later. You may not recognize what caused it, but it'll come back. It won't overlook you.

The law of increasing returns is eternal, automatic, and it's working all the time. It's just as inexorable as the law of gravitation. Nobody in the world can circumvent it, go around it, or have it suspended for one moment. It's operating all the time. The law of increasing returns means that when you go out of your way to render more service and better service than you're paid to render, it's impossible for you *not* to get back more than you really did, because the law of increasing returns takes care of that. If you're working for a salary, the law takes care of it in additional wages, greater responsibilities, promotions, or opportunities to go into business for yourself. In a thousand and one different ways, it'll come back.

THE LAW OF COMPENSATION

It doesn't always come back from the source to which you rendered the service. Don't be afraid to render service to a greedy buyer or a greedy employer. It makes no difference to whom you render service. If you render it in good faith and in good spirit, and keep doing it as a matter of habit, it's equally impossible for you *not* to be compensated as it is to *be* compensated. Therefore, you don't have to be too careful about the person to whom you render it. In fact, apply this principle with *everybody*, no matter who it is—strangers, acquaintances, business associates, and relatives, too. Make it your business to render useful service to everyone, regardless of the shape, form, or fashion in which you touch them.

The only way you can increase the space that you occupy in the world— and I don't mean just the physical space, but also the mental and the spiritual space as well—will be determined by the quality and the quantity of the service that you render. In addition to the quality and the quantity, is the mental attitude in which you render it. Those are the determining factors as to how far you'll go in life, how much you'll get out of life, how much you'll enjoy life, and how much peace of mind you'll have.

SELF-PROMOTION

Self-promotion elicits the favorable attention of other people. If you're alert-minded and take notice, you'll find in any organization those people that are going the extra mile. You'll find out very quickly. And if you watch the procedure and the records of those people who are going the extra mile, you'll see that when there are promotions around, they're the ones that get them. They don't have to ask for them; it's not necessary at all. Employers *look* for people who will go the extra mile. It permits one to become indispensable in many different human relationships. It enables one to command more than the average compensation.

GIVING FEEDS THE SOUL

I want you to know that it also does something to your soul inside of you; it makes you feel better. And if there were no other reason in the world why you should go the extra mile, I'd say that would be adequate. There are a lot of things in life that cause us to have negative feelings or cause us unpleasant experiences and feelings. However, this is one thing that you can do for yourself that'll *always* give you a pleasant feeling. And if you'll go back through your own experiences, I'm sure you'll remember that you never did a kind thing for anybody without getting a great deal of joy out of it. Maybe the other fellow didn't appreciate it, but that's unimportant.

It's like love. To have loved, that alone is a great privilege. It makes no difference whatsoever whether your love was returned by the other person. You've had the benefit by the emotion of love itself. So it is by the principle of going the extra mile. It'll do something *to you*. It'll give you greater courage. It'll enable you to overcome inhibitions and inferiority complexes that you've been storing through the years. There is so much benefit available to stepping out and making yourself useful to somebody.

If you do something courteous or useful for somebody who is not expecting it, don't be too surprised when they look at you in a quizzical sort of way, as much as to say, "Well, I just wonder why you're doing that." Some people will be a little bit surprised when you go out of your way to be useful to them.

MENTAL AND PHYSICAL BENEFITS

Going the extra mile in all forms of service will lead to mental growth and physical perfection across all areas as well as greater ability and skill in one's chosen vocation. Whether you're delivering a lecture or making up your notebook, or filling your job, if it's something that you're going to do over and over again in your life, make up your mind that every time you do it, you will excel beyond all previous efforts on your part. In other words, become a constant challenge to yourself. See how quickly and how rapidly you will grow if you'll go at it in that way.

I have never delivered a lecture in my life that I didn't intend to deliver better than I did previously. I don't always do it, but that's my intention. It makes no difference what kind of an audience I have, whether I have a big class or a small class. I don't often have small classes, but when I do, I put just as much into a small class as a big one, not only because I want to be useful to my students, but because I want to grow and I want to develop. Out of effort, out of struggle, and out of the use of your faculties comes growth. It enables one to profit by the law of contrast. You won't have to advertise that one very much—it'll advertise itself—because the majority of people around you are *not* going to be going the extra mile, and that's all the better for you.

If everybody went the extra mile this would be a grand world to live in, but you wouldn't be able to cash in on this principle as definitely as you can now because you'd have a tremendous amount of competition. Don't worry. I can assure you you're not going to have it. You'll be in a class by yourself. There will be cases where people you work with or are associated with will be shown up for *not* going the first mile, let alone the second one, and they won't like that. Are you going to cry about that one and quit and go back to your old habits, just because the other fellow doesn't like what you're doing? Of course not.

It's your individual responsibility to succeed. That's your sole responsibility. You can't afford to let anybody's ideas, idiosyncrasies, or notions get in the way of your success. You can't afford to do that. You should be fair with other people, but beyond that, you're under no obligations to let anybody's opinions or ideas stop you from being successful. I'd like to see the person that could stop me from being successful. I'd love to see what he looks like, and I want you to feel that way about it, too. I want you to make up your mind that you're going to put these laws into operation and that you're not going to let anybody stop you from doing it. It leads to the development of a positive, pleasing mental attitude, which is among the more important traits of a pleasing personality—actually, not *among* the more important; it *is* the most important one. A positive mental attitude is the first trait of a pleasing personality.

It's a marvelous thing to know what you can do to change the chemistry of your brain so that you're positive instead of negative. Do you know how easy it is? It's as easy as getting in that frame of mind where you want to do something useful for the other fellow, without rendering service on the one hand and picking his pocket with the other. You're doing it just because of the goodness that you get *out* of doing it. You know that if you render more service and better service than you're paid to render, sooner or later you'll be paid for more than you do and you'll be paid willingly. That's the way the law works. That's the law of compensation. It's an eternal law, it never forgets, and it has a perfectly marvelous bookkeeping system. You may be sure that when you are giving out the right kind of service with the right kind of a mental attitude, you are piling up credits that'll come back to you multiplied, sooner or later.

UNLIMITED BENEFITS

Going the extra mile tends to develop a keen, alert imagination because it is a habit that keeps you continuously seeking new and more efficient ways of rendering useful service. The reason that's important is that, as you begin to look around to see how many places, and ways, and means there are in helping the other fellow to find *himself*, you find *yourself*.

One of the most outstanding things that I discovered in my research was that when you have a problem or an unpleasant situation you don't know how to solve, when you've done everything you know, and when you've tried every source you know of, and you're still at a stalemate, there is always one thing that you can do. I want to tell you that if you'll do that one thing, the chances are that you not only will solve your problem, but you'll also learn a great lesson. That one thing is to find somebody who has an equal or a greater problem and start where you stand, then and there, to help that *other* person. Lo and behold, it unlocks something in you. It unlocks cells of the brain, unlocking cells that permit Infinite Intelligence to come into your brain and give you the answer to the solution of your problem.

I don't know why that works, but do you know how I know that it *does* work? Do you know why I can make that statement so positive and not qualify it? I arrived at that decision by experience, by trying it out hundreds and hundreds of times myself, and by seeing it tried out hundreds and hundreds of times by my students to whom I have recommended that same thing. What a simple thing that is! I don't know *what it does* and I don't know *why it works*. There are a lot of things in life I don't know and there are a lot of things you don't know. There are also some things that you do know that you don't do much about. This is one of those things that I don't know anything about but I do something about.

I follow the law because I know that if I need my own mind to be opened up to receive opportunity, the best way in the world to open it up is to start looking around to see how many other people I can help.

PERSONAL INITIATIVE

Personal initiative gets you into the habit of looking around for something useful to do and going out and doing it without somebody telling you to do it. That old man Procrastination is a sour old bird and he causes a lot of trouble in this world. People put off things until the day after tomorrow that they should have done the day before yesterday. Every one of us is guilty of it. I know I'm not free of it and I know you're not, either. But I can tell you I'm freer of it than I was a few years back. I can find a lot of things to do now and I find them because I get joy out of doing them. Anytime you're going the extra mile, you're going to get joy out of what you're doing; otherwise, you won't go the extra mile. It will help you develop the quality of personal initiative and help you overcome the quality of procrastination.

Going the extra mile also serves to build the confidence of others on one's integrity and general ability, and it aids one in mastering the destructive habit of procrastination. It develops definiteness of purpose, without which one cannot hope for success. That alone would be enough to justify it. It gives you an objective, so that you don't go around and around in circles like a goldfish in a bowl, always coming back to where you started with something that you didn't start out with. Definiteness of purpose comes out of this business of going the extra mile. It also enables you to make your work a joy instead of a burden—you get to where you love it. If you're not engaged in a labor of love, you're wasting a lot of your time.

One of the greatest joys in the world is being permitted to engage in the thing that you would rather do than all other things. When you're going the extra mile, you're doing just exactly that. You don't have to do it, nobody expects you to do it, and nobody asks you to do it. Certainly no employer would ask his employees to go the extra mile. He might ask for extra help once in a while, but he wouldn't do it as a regular thing. It's something that you do on your own initiative, and it gives a dignity to your labor. Even if you're digging a ditch, you're *helping* somebody, and there's a certain dignity to that which takes the fatigue and the unpleasantness out of the labor.

Going the extra mile often gives the greatest amount of joy. You might think you go the extra mile being married, but what about before you get married? Believe me, I spent a lot of time burning midnight oil and I didn't consider it hard work at all. It was my own idea and I used my initiative, but I also got a lot of joy out of doing it and I made it pay off. When you're courting the girl of your choice (or being courted by the man of your choice), it's marvelous how much sleep you can lose and still not be seriously hurt by it. Wouldn't it be a wonderful thing if you could put the same attitude into your relations with people professionally or in the business that you put into courtship? We're going to start sparking again.

It's going to start at home, with our own mates. I couldn't begin to tell you the number of married couples that I've started in on a new sparking spree. They're getting a lot of joy out of it. It saves a lot of friction and a lot of argument. It cuts down expenses. Go ahead and laugh, but it will do you good.

I don't mean to be facetious. I'm very serious when I

say that there is one of the finest places in the world to start going the extra mile. When you start going the extra mile with somebody that you haven't seen, sit down and have a little sales talk with them. Tell them that you've changed your attitude and you want a mutual agreement for both parties to change the attitude so that from here on out, *all* of us are going the extra mile. We're going to relate together on a different basis, where we'll all get joy out of it, more peace of mind, and more happiness in living. Wouldn't it be a wonderful thing if you went home tonight and had that kind of speech with your mate? It wouldn't hurt; it might help. Your mate might not be impressed by it, but you will be. Nothing will hinder you from enjoying it.

What about that person in business that you haven't been getting along so well with? Why not go in tomorrow morning with a smile and walk over to him or her and shake his hand and say, "Now look here and listen up, pal. From here on out, let's you and I enjoy working together." What would he say? It wouldn't work, huh? Oh, yes, it would. You try it and see. There's another thing that we have called pride, and if there's one thing that does more damage in this world than any other one, it's that little thing called pride. Don't be afraid. Don't be afraid to humiliate yourself if it's going to build better human relations with the people that you have to associate with all the time.

ESTABLISH OBLIGATION

Going the extra mile is the only thing that gives one the right to ask for promotions or more pay. Did you ever stop to think about that? You don't have a leg to stand on if you go to the purchaser of your services and ask for more money or for promotion to a better job unless, for some time previously, you have been going the extra mile and doing more than you're paid for. Obviously, if you're doing no more than you're paid for, then you're being paid for all you're entitled to, aren't you? Certainly, you are. So you have to first start going the extra mile and put the other fellow under obligation to you before you can ask any favors of him. And if you have enough people whom you have put under obligations to you by going the extra mile, when you need some favor, you can always turn in one direction or other and get it. It's a nice thing to know that you have that kind of credit hanging around, isn't it? I want you to have that kind of credit with other people and I want to teach you the technique by which you can do that.

NATURE GOES THE EXTRA MILE

We get our cue as to the soundness of the principle of going the extra mile by observing nature, and there's quite a bit of illustration regarding that. You will see that nature goes the extra mile by producing not only enough of everything for her needs but also a surplus for emergencies and waste. It shows this by the blooms on the trees and the fishes in the seas. She doesn't just produce enough fish to perpetuate the species; she produces enough to feed the snakes and the alligators and everything else. She produces those that die of natural causes, and even more, so there's enough to perpetuate the species. Nature is most bountiful in her business of going the extra mile, and in return, she is very demanding in seeing that every living creature goes the extra mile. Bees are provided with honey as compensation for their services in fertilizing the flowers in which the honey is attractively stored.

But they have to perform the service to get the honey, and it must be performed in advance.

You've heard it said that the birds of the air and the beasts of the jungle neither weave nor spin, but they always live and eat. If you observe wildlife at all, you'll see they don't eat without performing some sort of service, without working or doing something before they can eat. Take a flock of common old cornfield crows, for instance. They have to be organized in order to travel in flocks. And they have sentinels to protect them and codes by which they warn one another. In other words, they have to do a lot of educating before they can even eat safely.

Nature requires man to go the extra mile if he's going to have food. All food comes out of the ground, and if he's going to have food, he's got to plant seed. He can't live entirely on what nature plants (at least not in civilized life). On islands where they're not civilized, I suppose they depend on eating raw coconuts and what have you, but in civilized life, we have to plant our food in the ground. We have to clear the ground first before we plow it, harrow it, fence it, protect it against predatory animals and so forth. All of that costs labor and time and money. All of that has to be done in advance or you're not going to eat. I wouldn't have any trouble at all selling this idea that nature makes everybody go the extra mile to a farmer, because he already knows it beyond any question of a doubt. He knows every minute of his life that if he doesn't go the extra mile, he doesn't eat and he doesn't have anything to sell. A new employee can't start going the extra mile and immediately demand top wages or the best job in the place. It doesn't work out that way. You have to establish a record, a reputation. You have to get yourself recognized and received before you can begin to put the pressure on to get compensation back. If you go the extra mile in the right sort of mental attitude, chances are a thousand to one you'll never have to ask for compensation for the service you render, because it'll be tendered to you automatically, in the way of promotions or increased salary.

LAW OF COMPENSATION

Throughout the whole universe, everything has been so arranged through the law of compensation (and so adequately described by Emerson) that nature's budget is balanced. Everything has its opposite equivalent in something else. Positive and negative in every unit of energy, day and night, hot and cold, success and failure, sweet and sour, happiness and misery, man and woman. Everywhere and in everything, one may see the law of action and reaction in operation. Everything you do, everything you think, and every thought that you release causes a reaction, on somebody else or on you as the person releasing the thought. Because when you release a thought, you're not through with it. Every thought that you express, silently even, becomes a definite part of the pattern of your subconscious mind.

If you store in that subconscious mind enough negative thoughts, you'll be predominantly negative. And if you follow the habit of releasing only the positive thoughts, your subconscious pattern will be predominantly positive, and you will attract to you all of the things that you want. If you're negative, you'll repel the things that you want and attract only the things you don't want. That's a law of nature, too. Going the extra mile is one of the finest ways that I know to educate your subconscious mind to attract to you the things you want and to repel the things you don't want.

It's an established fact that if you neglect to develop and apply this principle of going the extra mile, you will never become personally successful, and you will never become financially independent. I know it's sound because I've had a great privilege that you haven't had yet, but you will have, in time. I've had the privilege of observing a great many thousands of people, some of whom applied the principle of going the extra mile and some of whom did not. I've had the privilege of finding out what happened to those who did and those who didn't. And I know beyond any question of a doubt that nobody ever rises above the ordinary stations in life or mediocrity without the habit of going the extra mile. It just doesn't happen. If I had discovered one case, just one case where somebody went on to the top without going the extra mile, I would say then that there are exceptions, but I am in a position to say there are no exceptions because I have never found that one case. I can definitely tell you from my own experiences that I have never had a major benefit of any kind in the world that I didn't get as the result of going the extra mile.

I want you to become self-determining, so you can do these things without the help of anybody. The payoff will come to you when you can go out and do anything in this world that you want to do, and regardless of whether anybody wants you to do it or whether they want to help you or whether they don't, you can do it on your own. That's one of the grandest, most glorious feelings that I know—that whatever I want to do, I can do it. I don't have to ask anybody, not even my wife. But if I had to ask her, I would, because I'm on good terms with her.

PEACE OF MIND

Here's a little item now that's not to be sniffed at: peace of mind that I got out of all those twenty years of going the extra mile. Do you have any idea how many people there are in the world at any one time who are willing to do anything for twenty years in succession without getting something back out of it? Do you have any idea how many people there are in this world who are willing to do something for only three days in succession without being sure they're going to get something out of it?

You'd be surprised at how few there are.

We're looking at one of the grandest opportunities that a human being could possibly have, especially here in this country where we really can create our own destiny and where we can express ourselves any way we want. Speech is free, activities are free, and education is free. There's wonderful opportunity to go the extra mile in any direction you want to travel in life. And yet, most people are not doing it. I have seen a time when there were not so many people interested in the philosophy because they were prosperous. They were doing all right and they had no troubles to speak of. Today, almost everybody has troubles, or they think they do.

Do you know what I do instead of finding out what's wrong with the rest of the world? Do you know how I put in my time? I try to find out what I can do to correct this guy here. I have to eat with him, sleep with him, shave his face every morning, wash his face, and give him a bath now and then. You have no idea how many things I have to do for him! I have to live with the guy, twenty-four hours a day.

I put in my time trying to improve myself, and, through myself, I try to improve my friends and my students, by writing books, by delivering lectures, and by teaching in other ways. It pays off very much better than it would if I sat down and took the old newspapers and read all of the murder stories and all of the divorce scandals and everything that's blazoned across the pages every day. I'm still talking about this fellow Napoleon Hill, who didn't have sense enough to decline Andrew Carnegie's offer to work twenty years for nothing. His declining years will be years of happiness because of the seeds of kindness and help he has sown in the hearts of others.

If I had my life to live over again, I'd live it just exactly the way I have. I'd make all the mistakes I made. I'd make them at the time in life when I made them, early on so I'd have time enough to correct some of them. And that period during which I would come into peace of mind and understanding would be in the afternoon of life, not in the forenoon, because I couldn't take it. When you're young, you can take it. But when you pass the noon hour and you go into the afternoon, your energies are not as great as they were before. Your physical energy, and sometimes your mental capacity, is not as great. You can't take as much trouble as you can in your days of youth. And you haven't got so many years left to correct the mistakes that you made.

To have the tranquility and the peace of mind that I have today, in the afternoon of life, is one of the great joys that has come out of this philosophy. If you ask me what has been my greatest compensation, I would say that's it. There are so many people at my age, and even much younger than I, who haven't found peace of mind and never will. They never will, because they're looking for it in the wrong place. They're not doing anything about it; they're expecting somebody else to do something about it for them. Peace of mind is something that you've got to get for yourself. First of all, you've got to earn it. As to how anybody can get peace of mind, a few of you would be surprised where you have to really start looking for it. It's not where the average person is looking for it. It's not out there in the joys of what money will buy or out there in the joys of recognition and fame and fortune. You'll find peace of mind in the humility of the one individual's own heart.

I get peace of mind mostly through an "inner wall," a place I go within where the wall is as high as eternity. I go into meditation many times each day and there's where I get my real peace of mind. I can always withdraw into that inner wall area, cut out every earthly influence, and commune with the higher forces of the universe. Anybody can do that. You can do that. When you get through with this philosophy, you'll be able to do anything you want to do, just as well or better than anything I can do. I'm hoping that every student that I turn out will eventually excel me in every way that I know possible. Maybe through writing books, you'll take up where I left off and write better books than I wrote. Why not? I haven't said the last word in my books nor in my lectures, or in anything else. As a matter of fact, I'm just a student, a fairly intelligent student, I think, but just a student on the path. The only state of perfection that I have achieved (and which cannot be surpassed by anyone) is that I have actually found peace of mind, and how to get it.

Engage in at least one act of going the extra mile every day. You can choose your own circumstance, even if it's nothing more than telephoning an acquaintance and wishing him good fortune. You'll be surprised what'll happen to you when you begin to call up your friends that you have been neglecting for some time and just say, "You were on my mind. I was thinking about you, and I just wanted to call and say how do you do, and I hope you are feeling as good as I am." You'd be surprised at what that'll do to you and what it'll do to your friend, too. It doesn't have to be a close personal friend. It just has to be somebody you know. Or, maybe relieve a friend from duty for half an hour or so, or have a neighbor send over his children while he attends the movies, or do a little babysitting for one of your neighbors. If you're going to be at home anyway, with children of your own, maybe you know a neighbor who would like to get off and go down to the movies but can't get away from her children. The children may be noisy, and they'll probably fight with your children, but if you're a real diplomat, you'll keep them apart. She'll be under obligation to you, and you'll feel that you've really been kind by helping out somebody who otherwise wouldn't have had a little freedom. It'd be a nice thing for some of you people who don't have any children to say, "Why don't I come over and baby-sit for you while you go out? You and your husband can go on a little courtship. Let me come over and babysit for you while you go out to the movie or go to a show." You'll have to know your neighbors pretty well in order to do that. Certainly, most of you would have some neighbor that you could approach on some such basis, and they wouldn't think you were crazy.

It's not so much what you do to the other fellow. It's what you do to yourself by finding ways and means of going the extra mile in little ways. Did you know that both the successes in life as well as the failures are made up of little things? So little that they're often overlooked, because the things that make success are such small and seemingly insignificant things.

I know people who are so popular they couldn't have an enemy. One of them is my distinguished business associate, Mr. Stone. He always goes the extra mile and look how prosperous he is. Look how many people are going the extra mile for him. There are a lot of people who, if they didn't make good money working for Mr. Stone, they'd pay him a salary just to work for him. I've actually heard one say that he's become immensely wealthy himself working for Mr. Stone. He said, "If I didn't make money out of working for him, I'd pay him if I had to, just for the association with him." Mr. Stone's not different from you or me or anybody else, except in his mental attitude toward people and toward himself. He makes it his business to go the extra mile. Sometimes, people take advantage of that. They don't act fairly with him. I've seen that happen, but he doesn't worry about that too much. In fact, he doesn't worry about anything at all, period. He's learned to adjust himself to life in such a way that he gets great joy out of living and gets great joy out of people. Write a letter to some acquaintance, offering him encouragement. In your job, do a little more than you're paid to do, stay a little longer on the job, or make some other person a little happier.

Points to Remember

1. The reason behind the failure of the majority of people is that they give up easily.
2. Nature requests and demands that every living thing go the extra mile in order to eat, in order to live, and in order to survive.
3. The eternality of the law of increasing returns.

7

FAILURE MAY BE A BLESSING

Failure often becomes a blessing in disguise, because it turns people back from contemplated purposes which, had they been carried out, would have meant embarrassment or even total destruction. Failure often opens new doors of opportunity and provides one with useful knowledge of the realities of life, through the trial-and-error method. Failure often reveals the methods which will not work, and cures vain people of their conceits.

Failure of the British armies under Lord Cornwallis in 1781 not only gave the American Colonies their freedom, but probably saved the British Empire from total destruction in World Wars I and II.

The economic failures of the South, due to the loss of their slaves in the Civil War, eventually yielded the seed of an equivalent benefit in more ways than one:

1. The loss of slaves forced people to begin depending upon themselves, and thereby they developed personal initiative.
2. The loss forced the women of the South to become independent by taking their places alongside of men in business and in the professions.

3. And, at long last, American industry is rapidly moving southward, where labor, raw materials, fuel, and weather conditions are more favorable. Thanks to the personal initiative of the Southerners, they stopped hating the Yankees and began to sell the South to northern industry.

In due time the South may become the industrial center of the United States.

Dr. Alexander Graham Bell spent years of research looking for the means of creating a mechanical hearing aid for his hard-of-hearing wife. In his original purpose he failed, but the research yielded the secret of the long-distance telephone.

When radio first came into popularity, about 1920, the Victor Talking Machine Company became frightened because it appeared that radio would ruin the talking machine business. The chief engineer of the Victor Talking Machine Company discovered, *in the principle of radio itself,* the means by which better recordings could be made, and from that discovery was born a demand for talking machines, such as the company never would have known without the discovery.

Thomas A. Edison's first major failure came when his teacher sent him home from school with a note advising his parents that he could not take an education. This so shocked Edison that he acquired an education which enabled him to become a truly great inventor.

Also, Edison's partial deafness might have been considered by some people as a failure of major proportions, but he adapted himself to it in such a way that he developed the power to hear "from within," through his sixth sense. This was a strong factor perhaps in his ability to uncover so many of nature's secrets in his business of inventing.

The loss of my mother, who died when I was a very young lad, would have been considered by some people a handicap of major proportions, but it turned out differently. I was compensated for the loss of my mother with a stepmother whose influence upon me was so profound that she inspired me to engage in a calling whereby I have been able to serve others to a far greater extent than I might otherwise have done.

I felt that I had met with a major failure when a great uncle who was a multimillionaire (after whom I was named) died and left no portion of his fortune to me. I later had reason to be thankful I was left out of his will, for it became necessary for me to master poverty on my own account, through my own initiative, *and in doing so I learned the way to teach others how to master poverty.*

Analyze failure under whatsoever circumstances you choose and you will discover the profound truth that every failure brings with it the seed of an equivalent benefit. This does not mean that failure brings with it the full ripened fruit of an equivalent benefit, but only the seed which must be discovered, germinated and developed to fruition through one's personal initiative, imagination, and definiteness of purpose.

INEVITABILITY OF FAILURE

Most men would consider the loss of the use of their legs a failure of major proportions, but Franklin D. Roosevelt so related himself to such a loss that it gave him a determined spirit to get along with braces, and he seemed to have done very well for himself without the use of his legs. His *mental attitude* toward his affliction was such that he reduced his handicap to a minimum of inconvenience.

The failures of Abraham Lincoln in store-keeping, surveying, soldiering, and the practice of law, turned his talents in a direction which prepared him to become the greatest President the United States has ever known.

More than twenty major failures which I experienced during the early part of my career changed my path and guided me eventually into a field in which I can best serve others.

Clarence Saunders' failure as a store clerk yielded him an idea from which he made a profit of four million dollars in four years. That idea was the Piggly-Wiggly System of self-help grocery stores, which marked the beginning of the self-help store system now in operation on a widespread scale throughout the country.

Failure in physical health often diverts attention of the individual from his physical body to his brain power, and introduces him to the real "boss" of the physical body—the mind—and opens wide horizons of opportunity which he never would have known without the failure of health.

Milo C. Jones of Fort Atkinson, Wisconsin, made a bare living from his farm until he was stricken with paralysis and suffered total loss of the use of his body. Then he made a discovery which only such an affliction could have uncovered for him. He discovered that he had a mind and its possibilities of achievement were limited only by his desires and demands upon it, even without the use of his physical body. Through the aid of his mind he conceived the idea of making sausage from young hogs, named his product "Little Pig Sausage," and lived to become a multimillionaire.

The fact that Mr. Jones did not discover his fabulous source of riches while he had the full use of his physical body is something which provides food for profound thought. The great Law of Change had to throw Milo C. Jones at on his back and break up his old habits, by which he earned his living with his hands, in order to introduce him to his brain power, which he discovered to be infinitely greater than his brawn power.

Verily, nature never permits an individual to be deprived of any of his inborn rights and blessings without providing him with the potentials of an equivalent benefit in some form, as in the case of Milo C. Jones.

Failure is a blessing or a curse, depending upon the individual's reaction to it. If one looks upon failure as a sort of nudge from the Hand of Destiny which signals him to move in another direction, and if he acts upon that signal, the experience is practically sure to become a blessing. If he accepts failure as an indication of his weakness and broods over it until it produces an inferiority complex, then it is a curse. *The nature of the reaction* tells the story, and this is under the exclusive control of the individual always.

No one has complete immunity against failure, and everyone meets with failure many times during a lifetime, but everyone also has the privilege and the means by which he can react to failure in any manner he pleases.

Circumstances over which one has no control may, and they sometimes do, result in failure, but there are no circumstances which can prevent one from reacting to failure in a manner best suited for his benefit.

Failure is an accurate measuring device by which an individual may determine his weaknesses; and it provides therefore an opportunity for correcting them. In this sense failure always is a blessing.

Failure usually affects people in one or the other of two ways: It serves only as a challenge to greater effort or it subdues and discourages one from trying again.

The majority of people give up hope and quit at the first signs of failure, even before it overtakes them. And a large percentage of people quit when they are overtaken by a single failure. The potential leader is never subdued by failure, but is always inspired to greater effort by it. Watch your failures and you will learn whether you have potentialities for leadership. Your reaction will give you a dependable clue.

If you can keep on trying after three failures in a given undertaking you may consider yourself a "suspect" as a potential leader in your chosen occupation. *If you can keep on trying after a dozen failures the seed of a genius is germinating within your soul.* Give it the sunshine of Hope and Faith and watch it grow into great personal achievements.

It appears that nature often knocks individuals down with adversities in order to learn who among them *will get up and make another fight!* Those who make the grade are chosen as people of destiny, to serve as leaders in work of great importance to mankind.

May I remind you that the next time you meet with failure, if you will remember that every failure and every adversity carries with it the seed of an equivalent benefit, and start where you stand to recognize that seed and begin to germinate it through action, you may discover that *there never is any such reality as failure until one accepts it as such!*

MANTRA FOR NEVER QUITTING

It would have been most natural and logical for Milo C. Jones to have accepted his affliction as a knockout blow from which he never would recover, and no one would have blamed him if he had done so, but he reacted to his handicap in a positive manner which yielded him a better working relationship with the power of his mind. His *reaction* was the important part of the experience, because it paid off in terms of financial riches such as he had never dreamed of acquiring.

Most so-called failures are only temporary defeats which can be converted into assets of a priceless nature if one takes a positive mental attitude toward them.

From birth until death, Life poses a constant challenge to people to master failure without going down for the count, and rewards with bountiful opulence and great personal powers those who successfully meet the challenge.

The world generously forgives one for his mistakes and temporary defeats, provided always he accepts them as such and keeps on trying, *but there is no forgiveness for the sin of quitting when the going is hard!*

Life's motto is: "A WINNER NEVER QUITS AND A QUITTER NEVER WINS!"

Japan's failure in World War II was her greatest victory, since that failure broke the vicious yoke of superstition by which the Japanese people had been bound, and gave them their first taste of democracy and an opportunity to take their place in the family of civilized peoples on an equality with all others.

In all human endeavors nature seems to favor the "fool" who did not know he could fail, but who went ahead and did the "impossible" before he discovered it couldn't be done.

Henry P. Kaiser had never built seaworthy ships, but the emergency of World War II called for more ships than the established ship-building sources could supply, so Mr. Kaiser began building ships with such faith and enthusiasm that he literally "ran rings" around some of the older and more experienced men in that business, with an all-time high in production and all-time low in cost!

The man who says "it can't be done" usually winds up under the feet of the man who is busy doing it— *the man who succeeds because he has thrown himself in the path of the laws of the universe and adapted himself to their habits,* and thereby insured himself against failure. The man who says "it can't be done" has never studied nature's laws.

An old miner spent thirty years in search of precious metals, only to meet with disappointment and despair until he was overtaken by the misfortune of having his trusty mule break its leg in a gopher hole. The mule had to be shot. While digging a hole in which to bury the animal the miner struck the richest copper deposit in the entire world!

Destiny often selects dramatic ways in which to reward people for stick-to-itiveness and the will to keep on trying in the face of defeat.

In this world of practical realism one must constantly remind himself that *our only limitations are those which we set up in our minds or permit others to establish for us.*

Henceforth and forever remember that no experience can be classified as a failure unless and until it has been accepted as such! Remember also, that only the person who meets with a given experience has the right to call it a failure, or some other name; that the verdict of all others is ruled out.

Points to Remember

1. Failure often leads to new opportunities.
2. Analyze your failures and determine your weaknesses.
3. Failure is a blessing or a curse, depending upon the individual's reaction to it.

8

LEARN TO SEE

When he was born, George W. Campbell was blind.

"Bilateral congenital cataracts," the doctor called it.

George's father looked at the doctor, not wanting to believe. "Isn't there anything you can do? Wouldn't an operation help?"

"No," said the doctor. "As of now, we know of no way to treat this condition."

George Campbell couldn't see, but the love and faith of his parents made his life rich. As a very young boy, he did not know that he was missing anything.

And then, when George was six years old, something happened which he wasn't able to understand. One afternoon he was playing with another youngster. The other boy, forgetting that George was blind, tossed a ball to him. "Look out! It'll hit you!"

The ball did hit George—and nothing in his life was quite the same after that. George was not hurt, but he was greatly puzzled. Later he asked his mother: "How could Bill know what's going to happen to me before I know it?"

His mother sighed, for now the moment she dreaded had arrived. Now it was necessary for her to tell her son for the first time: "You are blind." And here is how she did it:

"Sit down, George," she said softly as she reached over and

took one of his hands. "I may not be able to describe it to you, and you may not be able to understand, but let me try to explain it this way." And sympathetically she took one of his little hands in hers and started counting the fingers.

"One—two—three—four—five. These fingers are similar to what is known as the five senses." She touched each finger between her thumb and index finger in sequence as she continued the explanation.

"This little finger for hearing; this little finger for touch; this little finger for smell; this one for taste," and then she hesitated before continuing: "this little finger for sight. And each of the five senses, like each of the five fingers, sends messages to your brain."

Then she closed the little finger which she had named "sight" and tied it so that it would stay next to the palm of George's hand.

"George, you are different from other boys," she explained, "because you have the use of only four senses, like four fingers: one, hearing—two, touch—three, smell—and four, taste. But you don't have the use of your sense of sight. Now I want to show you something. Stand up," she said gently.

George stood up. His mother picked up his ball. "Now hold out your hand as if you were going to catch this," she said.

George held out his hands, and in a moment he felt the hard ball hit his fingers. He closed them tightly around it and caught it.

"Fine. Fine," said his mother. "I never want you to forget what you have just done. You can catch a ball with four fingers instead of five, George. You can also *catch* and *hold* a full and happy life with four senses instead of five—if you get in there and keep trying." Now George's mother had used a metaphor, and such a simple figure of speech is one of the quickest and most effective methods of communicating ideas between persons.

George never forgot the symbol of "four fingers instead of five." It meant to him the symbol of hope. And whenever he became discouraged because of his handicap, he used the symbol as a self-motivator. It became a form of self-suggestion to him. For he would repeat "four fingers instead of five" frequently. At times of need it would flash from his subconscious to his conscious mind.

And he found that his mother was right. He was able to catch a full life, and hold it with the use of the four senses which he did have.

APPRECIATION FOR THE SENSE OF SIGHT

But George Campbell's story doesn't end here.

In the middle of his junior year at high school the boy became ill, and it was necessary for him to go to the hospital. While George was convalescing, his father brought him information from which he learned that science had developed a cure for congenital cataracts. Of course, there was a chance of failure but—the chances for success far outweighed those for failure.

George wanted so much to see that he was willing to risk failure in order to see.

During the next six months four delicate surgical operations were performed—two on each eye. For days George lay in the darkened hospital room with bandages over his eyes.

And finally the day came for the bandages to be removed. Slowly, carefully, the doctor unwound the gauze from around George's head and over his eyes. There was only a blur of light.

George Campbell was still technically blind!

For one awful moment he lay thinking. And then he heard the doctor moving beside his bed. Something was being placed over his eyes.

"Now, can you see?" came the doctor's question.

George raised his head slightly from the pillow. The blur of light became color, the color a form, a figure.

"George!" a voice said. He recognized the voice. It was his mother's voice.

For the first time in his 18 years of life George Campbell was seeing his mother. There were the tired eyes, the wrinkled, 62-year-old face, and the knotted and gnarled hands. But to George she was most beautiful.

To him—she was an angel. The years of toil and patience, the years of teaching and planning, the years of being his seeing eyes, the love and affection: that was what George saw.

To this day he treasures his first visual picture: the sight of his mother. And, as you will see, he learned an appreciation for his sense of sight from this first experience.

"None of us can understand," he says, "the miracle of sight, unless we have had to do without it."

Seeing is a learned process. But George also learned something that is very helpful to anyone interested in the study of PMA. He will never forget the day he saw his mother standing before him in the hospital room, and did not know who she was—or even what she was—until he heard her speak. "What we see," George points out, "is always an interpretation of the mind. We have to train the mind to interpret what we see."

This observation is backed up by science. "Most of the process of seeing is not done by the eyes at all," says Dr. Samuel Renshaw, in describing the mental process of seeing. "The eyes act as hands which reach 'out there' and grab meaningless 'things' and bring them into the brain. The brain then turns the 'things' over to the memory. It is not until the brain interprets in terms of comparative action that we really *see* anything."

Some of us go through life "seeing" very little of the power and the glory around us. We do not properly filter the information that our eyes give us through the mental processes of the brain. As a result we often behold things without really *seeing* them at all. We receive physical impressions without grasping their meaning to us. We do not, in other words, put PMA to work on the impressions that are sent to our brain.

Is it time to have your mental vision checked? Not your physical vision—that is a matter for the medical specialists. But mental vision, like physical vision, can become distorted. When it does you can grope in a haze of false concepts…bumping and hurting yourself and others unnecessarily.

The most common physical weaknesses of the eye are two opposite extremes—nearsightedness and farsightedness. These are the major distortions of mental vision, too.

The person who is mentally nearsighted is apt to overlook objects and possibilities that are distant. He pays attention only to the problems immediately at hand and is blind to the opportunities that could be his by thinking and planning in terms of the future. You are nearsighted if you do not make plans, form objectives, and lay the foundation for the future.

On the other hand, the mentally farsighted person is apt to overlook possibilities that are right before him. He does not see the opportunities at hand. He sees only a dream-world of the future, unrelated to the present. He wants to start at the top rather than move up step by step—and he does not recognize that the only job where you can start at the top is the job of digging a hole.

They looked and recognized what they saw. So, in the process of learning to see, you will want to develop both your near sight and your far sight. The advantages to the man who knows how to see what is directly in front of him are enormous. For years the people in the little town of Darby, Montana, used to look up at what they called Crystal Mountain. The mountain was given this name because erosion had exposed a ledge of a lightly sparkling crystal that looked something like rock salt. A pack trail was built directly across the outcropping as early as 1937. But it wasn't until the year 1951—14 years later—that anyone bothered to stoop down, pick up a piece of the sparkling material, and really look at it.

START SEEING MORE THAN WHAT YOU WANT TO SEE

It was in this year 1951 that two Darby men, Mr. A. E. Cumley and Mr. L. I. Thompson, saw a mineral collection displayed in the town. Thompson and Cumley became very excited. There in the mineral display were specimens of beryl which, according to the attached card, was used in atomic energy research. Immediately Thompson and Cumley staked claims on Crystal Mountain. Thompson sent a specimen of the ore to the Bureau of Mines office in Spokane, together with a request to send an examiner to see a "very large deposit" of the mineral. Later that year the Bureau of Mines sent a bulldozer up the mountain and scraped off enough of the outcropping to determine that here indeed was one of the world's greatest deposits of extremely valuable beryllium. Today, heavy earth-moving trucks struggle up the mountain and work their way back down again, weighted down with the extremely heavy ore, while at the bottom, virtually waiting with dollar bills in their hands, are representatives of the United States Steel Company and the United States Government, each anxious to buy the highly valued ore. All because one day two young men not only observed with their eyes, but took the trouble to see with their minds. Today these men are well on their way to being multimillionaires.

A mentally farsighted person could not have done what Thompson and Cumley did—if his mental vision were distorted. For he is the man who can see only far-off values while the advantages that lie at his feet go unclaimed. Are there fortunes right at your doorstep? Look about you. As you go about your daily chores are there small areas of irritation? Perhaps you can think of a way to overcome them—a way that will be helpful not only to yourself but to others. Many a man has made a fortune by meeting such homely needs. This was so of the man who invented the bobby pin and the one who devised the paper clip. It was so of the man who invented the zipper, and the metal pants-fastener. Look about you. Learn to see. You may find *Acres of Diamonds* in your own backyard.

But mental nearsightedness can be just as much of a problem as mental farsightedness. The man with this problem sees only what is under his nose, while more distant possibilities go unclaimed. He is the man who does not understand the power of a plan. He does not understand the value of thinking time. He is so busy with the problems that immediately confront him that he does not free his mind to range into the distance, reaching for new opportunities, seeking trends, getting the big picture.

Being able to see into the future is one of the most spectacular accomplishments of the human brain. Down in the heart of the citrus belt in Florida there is a little town called Winter Haven. The surrounding country is farmland. Certainly it would be considered by most people as an area entirely unsuited for a large tourist attraction. It is isolated. It has no beach, no mountains, only mile after mile of gently rolling hills with little lakes and cypress swamps down in the valleys.

But to this region came a man who "saw" these cypress swamps with an eye that others had not used. His name was Richard Pope. Dick Pope bought one of these old cypress swamps, put a fence around it, and has turned down offers of at least a million dollars for the world-famous Cypress Gardens.

Of course, it really wasn't as simple as that. All along the line Dick Pope had to "see" opportunities in his situation.

For instance, there was the question of advertising. Pope knew that the only way he would be able to draw the public into such an isolated place was through a barrage of advertising. But ads cost money. So what Dick Pope did was quite simple. He went into the popular photography business. He set up a photo supply house at Cypress Gardens, sold his visitors film, and then taught them how to take spectacular shots of the Garden. He hired skilled water skiers. He put them through intricate performances while over a loudspeaker he announced to the public exactly what camera settings they should use in order to catch the action. And then, of course, when these travelers went back home, the very best trip pictures were always of Cypress Gardens. They gave Dick Pope the very best kind of advertising there is—word-of-mouth recommendations, with pictures!

This is the kind of creative seeing that we all need to develop. We need to learn how to look at our world with fresh eyes—seeing the opportunities that lie all about us, but simultaneously looking into the future for the chances that are there.

Seeing is a learned skill. But like any skill it must be exercised.

See another person's abilities, capacities, and viewpoint. We may think we recognize our own talents; yet in this respect we may be blind. Let's illustrate with an example of a teacher who needed to have her mental vision checked. She was both nearsighted and farsighted. For she could not see either the present or the future potential abilities and capacities of her students, or their points of view.

Now everyone—the great and the near great—had to have a starting point. They weren't born brilliant and successful. As a matter of fact, some of our greatest men were regarded as quite stupid at times during their lives. It was not until they grasped a positive mental attitude and learned to comprehend their capabilities and envision definite goals that they started their climbs to success. But there was one young man, in particular, whom his teachers thought "a stupid, muddle-headed block-head."

The youngster sat and drew pictures on his slate. He looked about and listened to everybody else. He asked "impossible questions" but refused to reveal what he knew, even under the threat of punishment. The children called him "dunce," and he generally stood at the foot of his class.

And this boy was Thomas Alva Edison. You will be inspired when you read the life story of Thomas A. Edison. He attended primary school for a total period of less than three months. The teacher and his schoolmates told him that he was stupid. Yet, he became an educated man after an incident in his life prompted him to turn his talisman from NMA to PMA. He developed into a gifted person. He became a great inventor.

What was that incident? What happened to Edison that changed his whole attitude? He told his mother about hearing the teacher tell the inspector at school that he was "addled" and it wouldn't be worthwhile to keep him in school any longer. His mother marched off to school with him and told all within range of her voice that her son, Thomas Alva Edison, had more brains than the teacher or the inspector.

Edison called his mother the most enthusiastic champion a boy ever had. And from that day forward he was a changed boy. He said, "She cast over me an influence which has lasted all my life. The good effects of her early training I can never lose. My mother was always kind, always sympathetic, and she never misunderstood or misjudged me." His mother's belief in him caused him to view himself in an entirely different light. It caused him to turn his talisman to PMA and take a positive mental attitude regarding studying and learning. This attitude taught Edison to view things with deeper mental insight, that enabled him to comprehend and develop inventions which benefited mankind. Perhaps the teacher didn't see because the teacher wasn't genuinely interested in helping the boy. His mother was.

You have a tendency to see what you want to see.

START USING ALL SENSES TO SUCCEED

To hear does not necessarily imply attention or application. *To listen* always does. Throughout *Success Through a Positive Mental Attitude* we urge you to listen to the message. This means: *to see* how you can relate and assimilate the principle into your own life.

Perhaps you'd like to see how you can relate the principle of the following experience into your own life.

Dr. Roy Plunkett, a DuPont chemist, made an experiment. He failed. When he opened the test tube after the experiment, he observed that it apparently contained nothing. He was curious. He asked himself, "Why?" He didn't throw the tube away as others might have done under similar circumstances. Instead, he weighed the tube. And, to his surprise, it weighed more than a tube of like make and design. So, again, Dr. Plunkett asked himself, "Why?"

In searching for the answer to his questions, he discovered

that marvelous transparent plastic, tetrafluoroethylene, commonly known as Teflon. During the Korean War, the United States government contracted for DuPont's entire output.

When there is something you don't understand, ask yourself: "Why?" Look at it more closely. You may make a great discovery.

Ask yourself questions. Asking yourself or others questions about things that puzzle you may reward you richly. This very procedure led to one of the world's greatest scientific discoveries.

A young Englishman, while vacationing on his grandmother's farm, was relaxing. He was lying on his back under an apple tree and engaging in thinking time. An apple fell to the ground. This young man was a student of higher mathematics.

"Why does the apple fall to the ground?" he asked himself. "Does the earth attract the apple? Does the apple attract the earth? Does each attract the other? What is the universal principle involved?"

Isaac Newton used his power to think and he made a discovery. To see mentally is to think. He found the answers he was looking for; the earth and the apple attracted each other, and the law of attraction of mass to mass applies to the entire universe.

Newton discovered the law of gravitation because he was observant and sought the answers to what he observed. Another man, because he exercised his powers of observation and acted upon what he perceived, found happiness and great wealth. Newton asked himself questions. The other man sought expert advice.

He became wealthy because he accepted advice. In Toba, Japan, in the year 1869, when he was just eleven years old, Kokichi Mikimoto continued his father's business as the village noodle-maker. His father had developed an illness that prevented him from working. The youngster supported his six brothers, three sisters, and his parents. In addition to making the noodles daily, young Mikimoto had to sell them. He proved to be a good salesman.

Mikimoto had previously been tutored by a Samurai who taught:

Exemplification of true faith consists of acts of kindness and love for one's fellowmen, not mere formal prayers uttered by rote.

And with this basic PMA philosophy of positive action, Mikimoto became a *doer*. He developed the habit of converting ideas into reality.

At the age of twenty he fell in love with the daughter of a Samurai. The young man knew that his future father-in-law would not bless his daughter's marriage with a noodle-maker. Therefore, he was motivated to harmonize with this known power. He changed his occupation and became a pearl merchant.

Like many persons who achieve success in any part of the world, Mikimoto kept searching for specific knowledge that would help him in his new activity. He, like the great industrialists of our day, sought help from a university. Professor Yoshikichi Mizukuri told Mikimoto of a theory of one of the laws of nature that had never been proved.

The professor said: "A pearl is formed in an oyster when a foreign object, like a grain of sand, is stuck in the oyster. If the foreign object does not kill the oyster, nature covers the object with the same secretion that forms the mother-of-pearl in the lining of the oyster's shell."

Mikimoto was thrilled! He could hardly wait to get the answer to the question he asked himself, "Can I raise pearls by deliberately planting a tiny foreign object in the oyster and letting nature take its course?"

He converted a theory into a positive action once he learned to see.

Mikimoto had been taught to see by that university professor. And then he used the power of his imagination. He engaged in creative thinking. He used deductive reasoning. He decided that if all pearls were formed only when a foreign object entered the oyster, he could develop pearls by using nature's laws. He could plant foreign objects in the oysters and force them to produce pearls. He learned to observe and act and he became a successful man.

Now a study of Mikimoto's life indicates that he employed all the 17 success principles. For knowledge doesn't make you successful. But application of the knowledge will. *Action!*

Many of the ideas which come to us as we learn to see with fresh eyes will strike others as bold. These ideas can either frighten us or, if we act on them, make our fortunes. Here is another true story of pearls. This time the hero is a young American, Joseph Goldstone. He sold jewelry to Iowa farmers, door-to-door.

Then one day in the heart of the Depression he learned that the Japanese were producing beautiful cultured pearls. Here was quality, and it could be sold at a fraction of the cost of natural pearls!

Joe "saw" a great opportunity. In spite of the fact that it was a Depression year, he and his wife, Esther, converted all their tangible assets into cash and set out for Tokyo. They landed in Japan with less than $1,000—but they had their plan and lots of PMA.

They obtained an interview with Mr. K. Kitamura, head of the Japanese Pearl Dealers Association. Joe was aiming high. He told Mr. Kitamura of his plan for merchandising Japanese cultured pearls in the United States, and asked Mr. Kitamura for an initial credit of $100,000 in pearls. This was a fantastic sum, especially in a period of depression. After several days, however, Mr. Kitamura agreed.

The pearls sold well. The Goldstones were well on their way to becoming wealthy. A few years later, they decided they wanted to establish their own pearl farm, which they did with the help of Mr. Kitamura. Once again they "saw" opportunity where others had seen nothing. Experience proved that the mortality rate of oysters into which a foreign object had been artificially inserted was over 50 per cent.

"How can we eliminate this great loss?" they asked themselves.

After much study, the Goldstones began to use on the oysters the methods employed in hospital rooms. The outside shells were scraped and scrubbed to reduce the danger of infection to the oyster. The "surgeon" used a liquid anesthetic that relaxed the oyster. Then he slipped a tiny clam pellet into each oyster as a nucleus for the pearl that was to be formed. The incision was made with a sterilized scalpel. Then the oyster was put into a cage, and the cage was dropped back into the water. Every four months cages were raised and the oysters were given a physical checkup. Through these techniques, 90 per cent of the oysters lived and developed pearls, and the Goldstones went on to acquire a fabulous fortune.

Time and again we see how men and women have become successful after they learned to apply mental perception. The ability to see is much more than the physical process of taking light rays through the retina of the eye. It is the skill of interpreting what you see and applying that interpretation to your life and the lives of others.

Learning to see will bring to you opportunities that you never dreamed existed. However, there is more to success through PMA than learning mental perception. You must also learn to act on what you learn. Action is important because through action you get things done.

Don't wait any longer. Read "The Secret of Getting Things Done," the next chapter, and move another rung up the ladder of success through PMA.

> **Points to Remember**
>
> 1. Hope as a self-motivator.
> 2. What we see is always an interpretation of the mind.
> 3. Start seeing beyond what reaches the eye.

9

SELF-CONFIDENCE

Skepticism is the deadly enemy of progress and self-development. You might as well lay this book aside and stop right here as to approach this lesson with the feeling that it was written by some longhaired theorist who had never tested the principles upon which the lesson is based.

Surely this is no age for the skeptic, because it is an age in which we have seen more of Nature's laws uncovered and harnessed than had been discovered in all past history of the human race. Within three decades we have witnessed the mastery of the air; we have explored the ocean; we have all hut annihilated distances on the earth; we have harnessed the lightning and made it turn the wheels of industry; we have made seven blades of grass grow where but one grew before; we have instantaneous communication between the nations of the world. Truly, this is an age of illumination and unfoldment, but we have as yet barely scratched the surface of knowledge. However, when we shall have unlocked the gate that leads to the secret power which is stored up within us it will bring us knowledge that will make all past discoveries pale into oblivion by comparison.

Thought is the most highly organized form of energy known to man, and this is an age of experimentation and research that is sure to bring us into greater understanding of that mysterious force called thought, which reposes within us. We have already found out enough about the human mind to know that a man may throw off the accumulated effects of a thousand generations of *fear*, through the aid of the principle of *Autosuggestion*. We have already discovered the fact that fear is the chief reason for poverty and failure and misery that takes on a thousand different forms. We have already discovered the fact that the man who masters *fear* may march on to successful achievement in practically any undertaking, despite all efforts to defeat him.

The development of self-confidence starts with the elimination of this demon called fear, which sits upon a man's shoulder and whispers into his ear, *"You can't do it—you are afraid to try—you are afraid of public opinion—you are afraid that you will fail—you are afraid you have not the ability."*

This *fear* demon is getting into close quarters. Science has found a deadly weapon with which to put it to flight, and this lesson on *self-confidence* has brought you this weapon for use in your battle with the world-old enemy of progress, *fear*.

THE SIX BASIC FEARS OF MANKIND

Every person falls heir to the influence of six basic fears. Under these six fears may be listed the lesser fears. The six basic or major fears are here enumerated and the sources from which they are believed to have grown are described. The six basic fears are:

- a. The fear of Poverty
- b. The fear of Old Age
- c. The fear of Criticism
- d. The fear of Loss of Love of Someone

e. The fear of Ill Health
f. The fear of Death.

Study the list, then take inventory of your own fears and ascertain under which of the six headings you can classify them.

Every human being who has reached the age of understanding is bound down, to some extent, by one or more of these six basic fears. As the first step in the elimination of these six evils let us examine the sources from whence we inherited them.

PHYSICAL AND SOCIAL HEREDITY

All that man is, both physically and mentally, he came by through two forms of heredity. One is known as physical heredity and the other is called social heredity.

Through the law of physical heredity man has slowly evolved from the amoeba (a single-cell animal form), through stages of development corresponding to all the known animal forms now on this earth, including those which are known to have existed but which are now extinct.

Every generation through which man has passed has added to his nature something of the traits, habits and physical appearance of that generation. Man's physical inheritance, therefore, is a heterogeneous collection of many habits and physical forms.

There seems little, if any, doubt that while the six basic fears of man could not have been inherited through physical heredity (these six basic fears being mental states of mind and therefore not capable of transmission through physical heredity), it is obvious that through physical heredity a most favorable lodging place for these six fears has been provided.

For example, it is a well-known fact that the whole process of physical evolution is based upon death, destruction, pain and cruelty; that the elements of the soil of the earth find transportation, in their upward climb through evolution, based upon the death of one form of life in order that another and higher form may subsist. All vegetation lives by "eating" the elements of the soil and the elements of the air. All forms of animal life live by "eating" some other and weaker form, or some form of vegetation.

The cells of all vegetation have a very high order of intelligence. The cells of all animal life likewise have a very high order of intelligence.

Undoubtedly the animal cells of a fish have learned, out of bitter experience, that the group of animal cells known as a fish hawk are to be greatly feared.

By reason of the fact that many animal forms (including that of most men) live by eating the smaller and weaker animals, the "cell intelligence" of these animals which enter into and become a part of man brings with it the FEAR growing out of their experience in having been eaten alive.

This theory may seem to be far-fetched, and in fact it may not be true, but it is at least a logical theory if it is nothing more. The author makes no particular point of this theory, nor does he insist that it accounts for any of the six basic fears. There is another, and a much better explanation of the source of these fears, which we will proceed to examine, beginning with a description of social heredity.

By far the most important part of man's make-up comes to him through the law of social heredity, this term having reference to the methods by which one generation imposes upon the minds of the generation under its immediate control the superstitions, beliefs, legends and ideas which it, in turn, inherited from the generation preceding.

The term "social heredity" should be understood to mean

any and all sources through which a person acquires knowledge, such as schooling of religious and all other natures; reading, word of mouth conversation, story telling and all manner of thought inspiration coming from what is generally accepted as one's "personal experiences."

Through the operation of the law of social heredity anyone having control of the mind of a child may, through intense teaching, plant in that child's mind any idea, whether false or true, in such a manner that the child accepts it as true and it becomes as much a part of the child's personality as any cell or organ of its physical body (and just as hard to change in its nature).

It is through the law of social heredity that the religionist plants in the child mind dogmas and creeds and religious ceremonies too numerous to describe, holding those ideas before that mind until the mind accepts them and forever seals them as a part of its irrevocable belief.

The mind of a child which has not come into the age of general understanding, during an average period covering, let us say, the first two years of its life, is plastic, open, clean and free. Any idea planted in such a mind by one in whom the child has confidence takes root and grows, so to speak, in such a manner that it never can be eradicated or wiped out, no matter how opposed to logic or reason that idea may be.

Many religionists claim that they can so deeply implant the tenets of their religion in the mind of a child that there never can be room in that mind for any other religion, either in whole or in part. The claims are not greatly overdrawn.

With this explanation of the manner in which the law of social heredity operates the student will be ready to examine the sources from which man inherits the six basic fears. Moreover, any student (except those who have not yet grown big enough to examine truth that steps upon the "pet corns" of their own superstitions) may check the soundness of the principle of social heredity as it is here applied to the six basic fears, without going outside of his or her own personal experiences.

Fortunately, practically the entire mass of evidence submitted in this lesson is of such a nature that all who sincerely seek the truth may ascertain, for themselves, whether the evidence is sound or not.

For the moment at least, lay aside your prejudices and preconceived ideas (you may always go back and pick them up again, you know) while we study the origin and nature of man's Six Worst Enemies, the six basic fears, beginning with:

THE FEAR OF POVERTY

It requires courage to tell the truth about the origin of this fear, and still greater courage, perhaps, to accept the truth after it has been told. The fear of poverty grew out of man's inherited tendency to prey upon his fellow man economically. Nearly all forms of lower animals have instinct but appear not to have the power to reason and think; therefore, they prey upon one another physically. Man, with his superior sense of intuition, thought and reason, does not eat his fellow men bodily; he gets more satisfaction out of eating them FINANCIALLY!

Of all the ages of the world of which we know anything, the age in which we live seems to be the age of money worship. A man is considered less than the dust of the earth unless he can display a fat bank account. Nothing brings man so much suffering and humiliation as does POVERTY. No wonder man FEARS poverty. Through a long line of inherited experiences with the man-animal man has learned, for certain, that this animal cannot always be trusted where matters of money and other evidences of earthly possessions are concerned.

Many marriages have their beginning (and oftentimes their ending) solely on the basis of the wealth possessed by one or both of the contracting parties. It is no wonder that the divorce courts are busy!

"Society" could quite properly be spelled "Society," because it is inseparably associated with the dollar mark. So eager is man to possess wealth that he will acquire it in whatever manner he can; through legal methods, if possible, through other methods if necessary.

The fear of poverty is a terrible thing!

A man may commit murder, engage in robbery, rape and all other manner of violation of the rights of others and still regain a high station in the minds of his fellow men, PROVIDING always that he does not lose his wealth. Poverty, therefore, is a crime—an unforgivable sin, as it were.

No wonder man fears it!

Every statute book in the world bears evidence that the fear of poverty is one of the six basic fears of mankind, for in every such book of laws may be found various and sundry laws intended to protect the weak from the strong. To spend time trying to prove either that the fear of poverty is one of man's inherited fears, or that this fear has its origin in man's nature to cheat his fellow man, would be similar to trying to prove that three times two are six. Obviously no man would ever fear poverty if he had any grounds for trusting his fellow men, for there is food and shelter and raiment and luxury of every nature sufficient for the needs of every person on earth, and all these blessings would be enjoyed by every person except for the swinish habit that man has of trying to push all the other "swine" out of the trough, even after he has all and more than he needs.

The second of the six basic fears with which man is bound is:

THE FEAR OF OLD AGE

In the main this fear grows out of two sources. First, the thought that Old Age may bring with it POVERTY. Secondly, and by far the most common source of origin, from false and cruel sectarian teachings which have been so well mixed with "fire and brimstone" and with "purgatories" and other bogies that human beings have learned to fear Old Age because it meant the approach of another, and possibly a much more HORRIBLE, world than this one which is known to be bad enough.

In the basic fear of Old Age man has two very sound reasons for his apprehension: the one growing out of distrust of his fellow men who may seize whatever worldly goods he may possess, and the other arising from the terrible pictures of the world to come which were deeply planted in his mind, through the law of social heredity, long before he came into possession of that mind.

Is it any wonder that man fears the approach of Old Age?

The third of the six basic fears is:

THE FEAR OF CRITICISM

Just how man acquired this basic fear it would be hard, if not impossible, definitely to determine, but one thing is certain, he has it in well developed form.

Some believe that this fear made its appearance in the mind of man about the time that politics came into existence. Others believe its source can be traced no further than the first meeting of an organization of females known as a "Woman's Club." Still another school of humorists charges the origin to the contents of the Holy Bible, whose pages abound with some very vitriolic and violent forms of criticism. If the latter claim is correct, and those who believe literally all they find in the Bible are not mistaken, then God is responsible for man's inherent fear of Criticism, because God caused the Bible to be written.

This author, being neither a humorist nor a "prophet," but just an ordinary workaday type of person, is inclined to attribute the basic fear of Criticism to that part of man's inherited nature which prompts him not only to take away his fellow man's goods and wares, but to justify his action by CRITICISM of his fellow man's character.

The fear of Criticism takes on many different forms, the majority of which are petty and trivial in nature, even to the extent of being childish in the extreme.

Bald-headed men, for example, are bald for no other reason than their fear of Criticism. Heads become bald because of the protection of hats with tight fitting bands which cut off the circulation at the roots of the hair. Men wear hats, not because they actually need them for the sake of comfort, but mainly because "everybody's doing it," and the individual falls in line and does it also, lest some other individual CRITICIZE him.

Women seldom have bald heads, or even thin hair, because they wear hats that are loose, the only purpose of which is to make an appearance.

But it must not be imagined that women are free from the fear of Criticism associated with hats. If any woman claims to be superior to man with reference to this fear, ask her to walk down the street wearing a hat that is one or two seasons out of style!

The makers of all manner of clothing have not been slow

to capitalize this basic fear of Criticism with which all mankind is cursed. Every season, it will be observed, the "styles" in many articles of wearing apparel change. Who establishes the "styles"? Certainly not the purchaser of clothes, but the manufacturer of clothes. Why does he change the styles so often? Obviously this change is made so that the manufacturer can sell more clothes.

For the same reason the manufacturers of automobiles (with a few rare and very sensible exceptions) change styles every season.

The manufacturer of clothing knows how the man-animal fears to wear a garment which is one season out of step with "that which they are all wearing now."

Is this not true? Does not your own experience back it up? We have been describing the manner in which people behave under the influence of the fear of Criticism as applied to the small and petty things of life. Let us now examine human behavior under this fear when it affects people in connection with the more important matters connected with human intercourse. Take, for example, practically any person who has reached the age of "mental maturity" (from thirty-five to forty-five years of age, as a general average), and if you could read his or her mind you would find in that mind a very decided disbelief of and rebellion against most of the fables taught by the majority of the religionists. Powerful and mighty is the fear of CRITICISM!

The time was, and not so very long ago at that, when the word "infidel" meant ruin to whomsoever it was applied. It is seen, therefore, that man's fear of CRITICISM is not without ample cause for its existence.

The fourth basic fear is that of:

THE FEAR OF LOSS OF LOVE OF SOMEONE

The source from which this fear originated needs but little description, for it is obvious that it grew out of man's nature to steal his fellow man's mate; or at least to take liberties with her, unknown to her rightful "lord" and master. By nature all men are polygamous, the statement of a truth which will, of course, bring denials from those who are either too old to function in a normal way sexually, or have, from some other cause, lost the contents of certain glands which are responsible for man's tendency toward the plurality of the opposite sex.

There can be but little doubt that jealousy and all other similar forms of more or less mild dementia praecox (insanity) grew out of man's inherited fear of the Loss of Love of Someone.

Of all the "sane fools" studied by this author, that represented by a man who has become jealous of some woman, or that of a woman who has become jealous of some man, is the oddest and strangest. The author, fortunately, never had but one case of personal experience with this form of insanity, but from that experience he learned enough to justify him in stating that the fear of the Loss of Love of Someone is one of the most painful, if not in fact the most painful, of all the six basic fears. And it seems reasonable to add that this fear plays more havoc with the human mind than do any of the other six basic fears, often leading to the more violent forms of permanent insanity.

The fifth basic fear is that of:

THE FEAR OF ILL HEALTH

This fear has its origin, to considerable extent also, in the same sources from which the fears of Poverty and Old Age are derived.

The fear of Ill Health must needs be closely associated with both Poverty and Old Age, because it also leads toward the border line of "terrible worlds" of which man knows not, but of which he has heard some discomforting stories.

The author strongly suspects that those engaged in the business of selling good health methods have had considerable to do with keeping the fear of Ill Health alive in the human mind.

For longer than the record of the human race can be relied upon, the world has known of various and sundry forms of therapy and health purveyors. If a man gains his living from keeping people in good health it seems but natural that he would use every means at his command for persuading people that they needed his services. Thus, in time, it might be that people would inherit a fear of Ill Health.

The sixth and last of the six basic fears is that of:

THE FEAR OF DEATH

To many this is the worst of all the six basic fears, and the reason why it is so regarded becomes obvious to even the casual student of psychology.

The terrible pangs of fear associated with DEATH may be charged directly to religious fanaticism, the source which is more responsible for it than are all other sources combined.

So-called "heathen" are not as much afraid of DEATH as are the "civilized," especially that portion of the civilized population which has come under the influence of theology.

For hundreds of millions of years man has been asking the still unanswered (and, it may be, the unanswerable) questions, "WHENCE?" and "WHITHER?" "Where did I come from and where am I going after death?"

The more cunning and crafty, as well as the honest but credulous, of the race have not been slow to offer the answer to these questions. In fact the answering of these questions has become one of the so-called "learned" professions, despite the fact that but little learning is required to enter this profession. Witness, now, the major source of origin of the fear of DEATH!

"Come into my tent, embrace my faith, accept my dogmas (and pay my salary) and I will give you a ticket that will admit you straightway into heaven when you die," says the leader of one form of sectarianism. "Remain out of my tent," says this same leader, "and you will go direct to hell, where you will burn throughout eternity."

While, in fad, the self-appointed leader may not be able to provide safe-conduct into heaven nor, by lack of such provision, allow the unfortunate seeker after truth to descend into hell, the possibility of the latter seems so terrible that it lays hold of the mind and creates that fear of fears, the fear of DEATH!

In truth no man knows, and no man has ever known, what heaven or hell is like, or if such places exist, and this very lack of definite knowledge opens the door of the human mind to the charlatan to enter and control that mind with his stock of legerdemain and various brands of trickery, deceit and fraud.

The truth is this—nothing less and nothing more—That NO MAN KNOWS NOR HAS ANY MAN EVER KNOWN WHERE WE COME FROM AT BIRTH OR WHERE WE GO AT DEATH. Any person claiming otherwise is either deceiving himself or he is a conscious impostor who makes it a business to live without rendering service of value, through play upon the credulity of humanity.

WORDS OF WISDOM FOR THE WIVES

I am going to digress and here and break the line of thought for a moment while recording a word of advice to the wives of men. Remember, these lines are intended only for wives, and husbands are not expected to read that which is here set down.

From having analyzed more than 16,000 people, the majority of whom were married men, I have learned something that may be of value to wives. Let me state my thought in these words:

You have it within your power to send your husband away to his work or his business or his profession each day with a feeling of Self-confidence that will carry him successfully over the rough spots of the day and bring him home again, at night, smiling and happy. One of my acquaintances of former years married a woman who had a set of false teeth. One day his wife dropped her teeth and broke the plate. The husband picked up the pieces and began examining them. He showed such interest in them that his wife said:

"You could make a set of teeth like those if you made up your mind to do it."

This man was a farmer whose ambitions had never carried him beyond the bounds of his little farm until his wife made that remark. She walked over and laid her hand on his shoulder and encouraged him to try his hand at dentistry. She finally coaxed him to make the start, and today he is one of the most prominent and successful dentists in the state of Virginia. I know him well, for he is my father!

No one can foretell the possibilities of achievement available to the man whose wife stands at his back and urges him on to bigger and better endeavor, for it is a well-known fact that a woman can arouse a man so that he will perform almost superhuman feats. It is your right and your duty to encourage your husband and urge him on in worthy undertakings until he shall have found his place in the world. You can induce him to put forth greater effort than can any other person in the world. Make him believe that nothing within reason is beyond his power of achievement and you will have rendered him a service that will go a long way toward helping him win in the battle of life.

One of the most successful men in his line in America gives entire credit for his success to his wife. When they were first married she wrote a creed which he signed and placed over his desk. This is a copy of the creed:

> I believe in myself. I believe in those who work with me. I believe in my employer. I believe in my friends. I believe in my family. I believe that God will lend me everything I need with which to succeed if I do my best to earn it through faithful and honest service. I believe in prayer and I will never close my eyes in sleep without praying for divine guidance to the end that I will be patient with other people and tolerant with those who do not believe as I do. I believe that success is the result of intelligent effort and does not depend upon luck or sharp practices or double-crossing friends, fellow men or my employer.
>
> I believe I will get out of life exactly what I put into it, therefore I will be careful to conduct myself toward others as I would want them to act toward me. I will not slander those whom I do not like. I will not slight my work no matter what I may see others doing. I will render the best service of which I am capable because I have pledged myself to succeed in life and I know that success is always the result of conscientious and efficient

effort. Finally, I will forgive those who offend me because I realize that I shall sometimes offend others and I will need their forgiveness.

Signed ....

The woman who wrote this creed was a practical psychologist of the first order. With the influence and guidance of such a woman as a helpmate any man could achieve noteworthy success.

Analyze this creed and you will notice how freely the personal pronoun is used. It starts off with the affirmation of Self-confidence, which is perfectly proper. No man could make this creed his own without developing the positive attitude that would attract to him people who would aid him in his struggle for success.

This would be a splendid creed for every salesman to adopt. It might not hurt your chances for success if *you* adopted it. Mere adoption, however, is not enough. You must *practice* it! Read it over and over until you know it by heart. Then repeat it at least once a day until you have literally transformed it into your mental make-up. Keep a copy of it before you as a daily reminder of your pledge to practice it. By doing so you will be making efficient use of the principle of Autosuggestion as a means of developing Self-confidence. Never mind what anyone may say about your procedure. Just remember that it is your business to succeed, and this creed, if mastered and applied, will go a long way toward helping you.

You might well remember that *Nothing can bring you success but yourself.* Of course you will need the co-operation of others if you aim to attain success of a far-reaching nature, but you will never get that cooperation unless you vitalize your mind with the positive attitude of Self-confidence.

We come, now, to the point at, which you are ready to take hold of the principle of Autosuggestion and make direct use of it in developing yourself into a positive and dynamic and self-reliant person. You are instructed to copy the following formula, sign it and commit it to memory:

SELF-CONFIDENCE FORMULA

First: I know that I have the ability to achieve the object of my *definite purpose*, therefore I *demand* of myself persistent, aggressive and continuous action toward its attainment.

Second: I realize that the dominating thoughts of my mind eventually reproduce themselves in outward, bodily action, and gradually transform themselves into physical reality, therefore I will concentrate my mind for thirty minutes daily upon the task of thinking of the person I intend to be, by creating a mental picture of this person and then transforming that picture into reality through practical service.

Third: I know that through the principle of Autosuggestion, any desire that I persistently hold in my mind will eventually seek expression through some practical means of realizing it, therefore I shall devote ten minutes daily to demanding of myself the development of the factors named in the lessons of this Reading Course.

Fourth: I have clearly mapped out and written down a description of my *definite purpose* in life, for the coming five years. I have set a price on my services for each of these five years; a price that I intend to *earn* and *receive*, through strict application of the principle of efficient, satisfactory service which I will render in advance.

Fifth: I fully realize that no wealth or position can long endure unless built upon truth and justice, therefore *I will engage in no transaction which does not benefit all whom it affects.* I will succeed by attracting to me the forces I wish to use, and the co-operation of other people. I will induce others to serve me because I will first serve them. I will eliminate hatred, envy, jealousy, selfishness and cynicism by developing love for all humanity, because I know that a negative attitude toward others can never bring me success. I will cause others to *believe in me* because I will believe in them and in myself.

I will sign my name to this formula, commit it to memory and repeat it aloud once a day with full *faith* that it will gradually influence my entire life so that I will become a successful and happy worker in my chosen field of endeavor.

Signed ....

Before you sign your name to this formula make sure that you intend to carry out its instructions. Back of this formula lies a law that no man can explain. The psychologists refer to this law as Autosuggestion and let it go at that, but you should bear in mind one point about which there is no uncertainty, and that is the fact that whatever this law is it *actually works!*

Another point to be kept in mind is the fact that, just as electricity will turn the wheels of industry and serve mankind in a million other ways, or snuff out life if wrongly applied, so will this principle of Autosuggestion lead you up the mountain-side of peace and prosperity, or down into the valley of misery and poverty, according to the application you make of it. If you fill your mind with doubt and unbelief in your ability to achieve, then the principle of Autosuggestion takes this spirit of unbelief and sets it up in your subconscious mind as your dominating thought and slowly but surely draws you into the whirlpool of *failure*. But, if you fill your mind with radiant Self-confidence, the principle of Autosuggestion takes this belief and sets it up as your dominating thought and helps you master the obstacles that fall in your way until you reach the mountain-top of *success*.

THE POWER OF HABIT

Having, myself, experienced all the difficulties that stand in the road of those who lack the understanding to make practical application of this great principle of Autosuggestion, let me take you a short way into the principle of habit, through the aid of which you may easily apply the principle of Autosuggestion in any direction and for any purpose whatsoever.

Habit grows out of environment; out of doing the same thing or thinking the same thoughts or repeating the same words over and over again. Habit may be likened to the groove on a phonograph record, while the human mind may be likened to the needle that fits into that groove. When any habit has been well formed, through repetition of thought or action, the mind has a tendency to attach itself to and follow the course of that habit as closely as the phonograph needle follows the groove in the wax record.

Habit is created by *repeatedly* directing one or more of the five senses of seeing, hearing, smelling, tasting and feeling, in a given direction. It is through this repetition principle that the injurious drug habit is formed. It is through this same principle that the desire for intoxicating drink is formed into a habit.

After habit has been well established it will automatically

control and direct our bodily activity, wherein may be found a thought that can be transformed into a powerful factor in the development of *Self-confidence*. The thought is this: *Voluntarily, and by force if necessary, direct your efforts and your thoughts along a desired line until you have formed the habit that will lay hold of you and continue, voluntarily, to direct your efforts along the same line.*

The object in writing out and repeating the Self-confidence formula is to form the habit of making *belief in yourself* the dominating thought of your mind until that thought has been thoroughly imbedded in your subconscious mind, through the principle of *habit*.

You learned to write by repeatedly directing the muscles of your arm and hand over certain outlines known as letters, until finally you formed the habit of tracing these outlines. Now you write with ease and rapidity, without tracing each letter slowly. Writing has become a *habit* with you.

The principle of habit will lay hold of the faculties of your mind just the same as it will influence the physical muscles of your body, as you can easily prove by mastering and applying this lesson on Self-confidence. Any statement that you repeatedly make to yourself, or any *desire* that you deeply plant in your mind through repeated statement, will eventually seek expression through your physical, outward bodily efforts. The principle of habit is the very foundation upon which this lesson on Self-confidence is built, and if you will understand and follow the directions laid down in this lesson you will soon know more about the law of habit, from firsthand knowledge, than could be taught you by a thousand such lessons as this.

You have but little conception of the possibilities which lie sleeping within you, awaiting but the awakening hand of vision to arouse you, and you will never have a better conception of those possibilities unless you develop sufficient Self-confidence to lift you above the commonplace influences of your present environment.

The human mind is a marvelous, mysterious piece of machinery, a fact of which I was reminded a few months ago when I picked up Emerson's Essays and re-read his essay on Spiritual Laws. A strange thing happened. I saw in that essay, which I had read scores of times previously, much that I had never noticed before. I saw more in this essay than I had seen during previous readings because the unfoldment of my mind since the last reading had prepared me to interpret more.

The human mind Is constantly unfo"Iin', like the petals of a flower, until it reaches the maximum of development. What this maximum is, where it ends, or whether it ends at all or not, are unanswerable questions, but the degree of unfoldment seems to vary according to the nature of the individual and the degree to which he keeps his mind at work. A mind that is forced or coaxed into analytical thought every day seems to keep on unfolding and developing greater powers of interpretation.

Down in Louisville, Kentucky, lives Mr. Lee Cook, a man who has practically no legs and has to wheel himself around on a cart. In spite of the fact that Mr. Cook has been without legs since birth, he is the owner of a great industry and a millionaire through his own efforts. He has proved that a man can get along very well without legs if he has a well developed Self-confidence.

In the city of New York one may see a strong able-bodied and able-headed young man, without legs, rolling himself down Fifth Avenue every afternoon, with cap in hand, begging for a living. His head is perhaps as sound and as able to think as the average.

This young man could duplicate anything that Mr. Cook,

of Louisville, has done, if *he thought of himself as Mr. Cook thinks of himself*

Henry Ford owns more millions of dollars than he will ever need or use. Not so many years ago, he was working as a laborer in a machine shop, with but little schooling and without capital. Scores of other men, some of them with better organized brains than his, worked near him. Ford threw off the poverty consciousness, developed confidence in himself, thought of success and attained it. Those who worked around him could have done as well had they *thought* as he did.

Milo C. Jones, of Wisconsin, was stricken down with paralysis a few years ago. So bad was the stroke that he could not turn himself in bed or move a muscle of his body. His physical body was useless, but there was nothing wrong with his brain, so it began to function in earnest, probably for the first time in its existence. Lying flat on his back in bed, Mr. Jones made that brain create a *definite purpose*. That purpose was prosaic and humble enough in nature, but it was *definite* and it was a *purpose*, something that he had never known before.

His *definite purpose* was to make pork sausage. Calling his family around him he told of his plans and began directing them in carrying the plans into action. With nothing to aid him except a sound mind and plenty of *Self-confidence,* Milo C. Jones spread the name and reputation of "Little Pig Sausage" all over the United States, and accumulated a fortune besides.

All this was accomplished after paralysis had made it impossible for him to work with his hands.

Where *thought* prevails power may be found!

Henry Ford has made millions of dollars and is still making millions of dollars each year because *he believed in Henry Ford* and transformed that belief into a *definite purpose* and backed that purpose with a definite plan. The other machinists who worked along with Ford, during the early days of his career, visioned nothing but a weekly pay envelope and that was all they ever got. They demanded nothing out of the ordinary of themselves. If you want to *get more* be sure to *demand* more of yourself. Notice that this demand is to be made on *yourself!*

Points to Remember

1. Skepticism is the deadly enemy of self-development.
2. Thought is the most highly organized form of energy known to man.
3. Fear is the chief reason for poverty and failure.

10

HOW TO FIND SATISFACTION IN YOUR JOB

No matter what your job may be—boss or employee; plant manager or factory worker; doctor or nurse; lawyer or secretary; teacher or student; housewife or maid—you owe it to yourself to find satisfaction in your job as long as you have it.

You can, you know. Satisfaction is a mental attitude. Your own mental attitude is the one thing you possess over which you alone have complete control. You can determine to find satisfaction in your job, and discover the way to do so.

You are more apt to find satisfaction in your job if you do "what comes naturally"—that for which you have a natural aptitude or liking. When you take a job that doesn't "come naturally" you may experience mental and emotional conflicts and frustrations. You can, however, neutralize and eventually overcome such conflicts and frustrations—if you use PMA, and if you are motivated to gain experience to become proficient in the job.

Jerry Asam has PMA. And Jerry Asam loves his work. He finds satisfaction in his job.

Who is Jerry Asam? What does he do?

Jerry is a descendant of the Hawaiian kings. The job he

loves so much is that of sales manager for the Hawaiian office of a large organization.

Jerry loves his work because he knows his work well and is very proficient in it. Thus, he is doing what comes naturally. But even so, Jerry has days when things could be a little rosier. In sales work, days like this can be disturbing—if one does not study, think, and plan to correct difficulties and to maintain a positive mental attitude. So Jerry reads inspirational, self-help action books.

Jerry had read such inspirational books and learned very important lessons:

1. You can control your mental attitude by the use of self-motivators.
2. If you set a goal, you are more apt to recognize things that will help you achieve it than if you don't set a goal. And the higher you set your goal, the greater will be your achievement if you have PMA.
3. To succeed in anything, it is necessary to know the rules and understand how to apply them. It is necessary to engage in constructive thinking, study, learning, and planning time with regularity.

Jerry believed these lessons. He got into action. He tried them out himself. He studied his company's sales manuals, and practiced what he learned in actual selling. He set his goals—high goals—and achieved them. And each morning he said to himself: "I feel healthy! I feel happy! I feel terrific!" And he did feel healthy, happy, and terrific. And his sales results were terrific, too!

When Jerry was sure he himself was proficient in his sales work, he gathered about himself a group of salesmen and taught them the lessons he had learned. He trained the men in the latest and best selling methods as set forth in his company's training manuals. He took them out personally and demonstrated how easy it is to sell if one uses the right methods, has a plan, and approaches each day with a positive mental attitude. He taught them to set high sales goals and to achieve them with PMA.

Every morning Jerry's group meets and recites enthusiastically, in unison: "I feel healthy! I feel happy! I feel terrific!" Then they laugh together, slap one another on the back for good luck, and each one goes his way to sell his quota for the day. Each man sets a goal and he sets it so high that older, more experienced salesmen and sales managers on the mainland are amazed.

At the end of each week every salesman turns in a sales report that makes the president and sales manager of Jerry's organization smile big, broad smiles.

Are Jerry and the men under him happy and satisfied in their jobs? You bet they are! And here are some of the reasons they are happy:

1. They have studied their work well; they know and understand the rules and techniques and how to apply them so well that what they are doing comes naturally to them.
2. They set their goals regularly and they believe they will make them. They know that what the mind of man can conceive and believe, the mind of man can achieve with PMA.
3. They keep a positive mental attitude continually by using self-motivators.
4. They enjoy the satisfaction that comes with a job well done.

"I feel healthy! I feel happy! I feel terrific!"

HOW TO FEEL HAPPY, HEALTHY AND TERRIFIC

Another young salesman in the same organization on the mainland learned to control his mental attitude through the use of Jerry Asam's self-motivator. He was an eighteen-year-old college student who was working during his summer vacation selling insurance on a cold-canvass basis in stores and offices. Some of the things he had learned during his theoretical training period were:

1. The habits that a salesman develops within the first two weeks after leaving the sales school will follow him throughout his career.
2. When you have a sales target—keep trying until you hit it.
3. Aim higher.
4. In your moment of need, use self-motivators such as: *I feel healthy! I feel happy! I feel terrific!* to motivate yourself to positive action in the desired direction.

After he had a few weeks' selling experience, he set a specific target of achievement. He aimed to win an award. To qualify, it was necessary to make a minimum of one hundred sales in a single week.

By Friday night of that week, he had succeeded in making eighty sales—twenty short of his target. The young salesman was determined that nothing would stop him from achieving his objective. He believed what he had been taught: *What the mind of man can conceive and believe, the mind of man can achieve with PMA.* Although the other salesmen in his group closed their week's work on Friday night, he was back on the job early Saturday morning.

By three o'clock in the afternoon, he hadn't made a sale.

He had been taught that sales are contingent upon the attitude of the salesman—not the prospect.

He remembered the Jerry Asam self-motivator and repeated it five times with enthusiasm. *I feel healthy! I feel happy! I feel terrific!*

About five o'clock that afternoon he had made three sales. He was only seventeen from his goal. He remembered that *success is achieved by those who try and maintained by those who keep trying with PMA!* Again he repeated several times with enthusiasm, *I feel healthy! I feel happy! I feel terrific!* About eleven o'clock that night—he was tired, but he was happy! He had made his twentieth sale for the day! He had hit his target! He had won the award and learned that failure can be turned to success by—keeping on trying.

Mental attitude makes the difference. So it was mental attitude that motivated Jerry Asam and the salesmen under him to find satisfaction in their jobs. It was a controlled positive mental attitude which helped the young student earn the reward and satisfaction he sought.

Just look about you. Notice those people who enjoy their work and those who don't. What's the difference between them? Happy, satisfied persons control their mental attitude. They take a positive view of their situation. They look for the good, and when something isn't so good, they look first to themselves to see if they can improve it. They try to learn more about their work so that they can become more proficient and make their work more satisfying to themselves and their employer.

But those who are unhappy clutch their NMA tightly. Indeed, it is almost as if they want to be unhappy. They look for everything about which they can complain: the hours are too long; lunch hours are too short; the boss is too crabby; the company doesn't give enough holidays or the right kind of bonuses. Or maybe they even complain about irrelevant things, such as: Susie wears the same dress every day; John the bookkeeper doesn't write legibly, and so on, and so on. Anything—just so they can be unhappy. And they succeed very well, too. They are decidedly unhappy people—on the job and generally elsewhere, too. NMA possesses them entirely.

And this is true regardless of the type of work involved. If you want to be happy and satisfied, you can be: you will control your mental attitude and reverse your talisman from NMA to PMA; you will look for ways and means to create happiness.

If you can bring happiness and enthusiasm into your work situation, you'll be making a contribution that few others could equal. You will make your work fun and your job satisfaction will be measured in smiles—and in productivity, too.

THE STEP-STONE THEORY

A definite goal made her enthusiastic. In one of our classes, we were talking about this principle of bringing enthusiasm into one's job, when a young lady in the rear of the classroom raised her hand. She got to her feet and said:

"I've come here with my husband. What you say may be all right for a man in business, but it's no good for a housewife. You men have new and interesting challenges every day. But it's not like that with housework. The trouble with housework is…it's just too darned daily."

This seemed like a real challenge to us: there are a lot of people who have jobs that are "just too darned daily." If we could find some way to help this young lady, perhaps we could help others who thought their work was routine. We asked her what made her housework seem so "daily," and it turned out that she had no sooner finished making the beds when they were dirtied again, washing the dishes when they were soiled again, cleaning the floors when they were muddied again. "You just get these things done so they can get undone," she said.

"It does seem frustrating," the instructor agreed. "Are there any women who do enjoy housework?"

"Well, yes, I guess there are," she said.

"What do they find in housework to interest them and keep them enthusiastic?"

After a moment's thought the young woman replied, "Maybe it's their attitude. They don't seem to think their work is confining; they seem to see something beyond the routine."

This was the crux of the problem. One of the secrets of job satisfaction is being able to "see beyond the routine." It is knowing that your work is *leading somewhere.* This is true whether you are a housewife or a file clerk, a gasoline pump operator or the president of a large corporation. You'll find satisfaction in routine chores only when you see them as stepping-stones. Each chore a stone, leading in a direction that you choose.

Use the step-stone theory. The answer, then, for this young housewife, was to find some goal which she really wanted to achieve, and to find a way to make her routine daily housework lead to the attainment of that goal. She volunteered the information that she had always wanted to take her family on a trip around the world.

"All right," the instructor said. "We'll settle on that. Now, set yourself a time limit. When do you want to go?"

"When the baby is twelve years old," she said. "That will be six years from now."

"Now, let's see. This will take a little doing. You'll need money, for one thing. Your husband will have to be able to take off for a year. You will have to plan an itinerary. You will want to study up on the countries you will be visiting. Do you suppose you can find a way to let bed-making, dish-washing, floor-scrubbing, and meal-planning be stepping-stones toward your goal?"

A few months later the lady in this story came to see us. It was apparent the minute she walked into the room that here was a woman who had succeeded proudly.

"It's amazing," she told us, "how well this stepping-stone idea has worked! I haven't found a single chore that doesn't fit in. I use my cleaning time as a thinking and planning time. Shopping time is a wonderful time to expand our horizons: I deliberately buy foods from other countries: foods that we will be eating on our trip. And I use the meal time as a teaching time. If we are having Chinese egg noodles, I read all I can find about China and its people, and then at dinner I tell the family all about them.

"Not one of my duties is dull or uninteresting to me anymore. And I know they never will be again, thanks to the *step-stone theory!*"

So no matter how humdrum or tiresome your job may be, if at the end of it you see a goal that you desire, that job can bring satisfaction to you. This is a situation which confronts many persons in all walks of life. One young man may want to be a doctor, but he has to work his way through school. The job he takes will be decided by many factors, such as hours, location, rate of pay, and so on. Aptitude will have little to do with it. A very intelligent, ambitious young man may end up behind a soda fountain, washing cars, or digging ditches. Certainly the job offers him no challenge or stimulation. It is merely a means to an end. Yet because he knows he is going where he wants to go, to him whatever strains the job may impose on him are worth the end result.

USE YOUR DISSATISFACTION AS A MOTIVATING TOOL

Sometimes, however, the price to be paid on a given job is too high in relation to the goal which it will purchase. And if such a job should happen to be yours, change your job. For if you are unhappy at your job, the poisons of this dissatisfaction spread into every phase of living.

If, however, the job is worth the price but you are still unhappy, develop *inspirational dissatisfaction.* Dissatisfaction can be positive or negative, good or bad, depending upon the circumstances. Remember: *A positive mental attitude is the right mental attitude in a given situation.*

Develop inspirational dissatisfaction! Charles Becker, former president of Franklin Life Insurance Company, says: "I would urge that you be dissatisfied. Not dissatisfied in the sense of disgruntlement, but dissatisfied in the sense of that 'divine discontent' which throughout the history of the world has produced all real progress and reform. I hope you will never be satisfied. I hope you will constantly feel the urge to improve and perfect not only yourself, but the world around you."

Inspirational dissatisfaction can motivate persons from sinner to saint, failure to success, poverty to riches, defeat to victory, and misery to happiness.

What do you do: when you make a mistake? when things go wrong? when misunderstandings develop with others? when you meet defeat? when everything seems black? when it appears that there is no way to turn? when it looks as if a satisfactory solution to your problem is impossible?

Do you: Do nothing and allow disaster to overtake you? Do you fold up? Become frightened? Run away?

Or, do you develop inspirational dissatisfaction? Do you

turn disadvantages into advantages? Do you determine what you want? Do you apply faith, clear thinking, and positive action, knowing that desirable results can and will be achieved?

Every adversity has the seed of an equivalent benefit. Isn't it true that in the past what seemed to be a great difficulty or an unfortunate experience has inspired you to success and happiness that might not otherwise have been achieved?

Inspirational dissatisfaction can motivate you to succeed. Albert Einstein was dissatisfied because Newton's laws didn't answer all his questions. So he kept inquiring into nature and higher mathematics until he came up with the theory of relativity... And from that theory the world has developed the method of breaking the atom, learned the secret of transmuting energy into matter and vice versa, and dared and succeeded to conquer space—and all sorts of amazing things we very likely would not have accomplished if Einstein had not developed inspirational dissatisfaction.

Now, of course, we are not all Einsteins, and what results from our inspirational dissatisfaction may not change the world. But it can change our world and we can move forward in the direction we want to go. Let us tell you what happened to Clarence Lantzer when he became dissatisfied with his job.

Was it worth it? Now Clarence Lantzer had been a streetcar conductor in Canton, Ohio, for years. And one day he woke up in the morning and decided that he didn't like his job. It was too much the same. He was sick and tired of it. The more Clarence thought about the matter, the more dissatisfied he became. And he seemed to be unable to quit thinking about it. His dissatisfaction grew almost to an obsession. Clarence was mightily dissatisfied.

But when you have worked for a company as long as Clarence had worked for his streetcar company, you don't just quit because you decide that you are unhappy. At least, not if you are interested in whether or not your bread will be buttered.

Besides, Clarence had taken the PMA Science of Success course, and he had learned that one could be happy on any job if one wanted to. The thing to do was to adopt the right attitude.

So Clarence decided to take a sensible view of the situation and see what he could do about it. "How can I be happier on the job?" he asked himself.

And he came up with a very good answer indeed. He decided that he would be happier if he made others happy.

Now there were many people whom he could make happy, for he met many folks on his streetcar every day. He had always been able to make friends readily, so he thought: "I'll use this trait to make each day a little brighter for every person who boards my car."

Clarence's plan was wonderful—the customers thought. They enjoyed his little courtesies and cheerful greetings immensely. And they were happier, and so was Clarence, as the result of his cheerfulness and consideration.

But his supervisor took the opposite attitude. So the supervisor called Clarence in and warned him to stop all this un-wonted affability.

But Clarence paid no attention to the warning. He was having a good time making others happy. And as far as he and the customers were concerned, he was making a terrific success of his job.

Clarence was fired!

MATCH YOUR SKILLS WITH YOUR JOB PROFILE

So Clarence had a problem—and that was good. At least, according to the PMA Science of Success course, it was good.

Clarence decided that perhaps he had better visit me (I was living in Canton at the time) and see how and why this problem was so good. He called me and arranged for an appointment the next afternoon.

"I've read *Think and Grow Rich*, Mr. Hill, and I've studied the PMA Science of Success, but somewhere I must have gotten off on the wrong track." And he told me what had happened to him. "Now what do I do?" he concluded.

I smiled. "Let's look at your problem," I said. "You were dissatisfied with your work as it was. You did exactly right. You tried to use your best asset, your friendly and affable disposition, to do a better job and get and give more satisfaction on the job. The problem arises from the fact that your superior didn't have the imagination to see the value of what you were doing. But that's wonderful! Why? Because now you are in a position to use your fine personality for even greater goals."

And I showed Clarence Lantzer that he could use his fine abilities and friendly disposition to much better advantage as a salesman than as a streetcar conductor. So Clarence applied for and got a job as an agent for the New York Life Insurance Company.

The first prospect Clarence called on was the president of the streetcar company. Clarence turned his personality loose on this gentleman and came out of the office with an application for a $100,000 policy!

The last time I saw Lantzer, he had become one of New York Life's biggest producers.

Are you a square peg in a round hole? The characteristics, abilities, and capacities that make you happy and successful in one environment may create an opposite reaction in another. You have a tendency to do well what you want to do.

You are called a "square peg in a round hole" when you

work or engage in activities that do not come naturally, and that are inwardly repellent. In such an unhappy situation you can change your position and place yourself in an environment that is pleasing to you.

It may not be feasible to change your position. You can then make adjustments in your environment to coincide with your characteristics, abilities, and capacities so that you will be happy. When you do this, you "square the hole." This solution will help change your attitude from negative to positive.

If you develop and maintain a burning desire to do so, you can even neutralize and change your tendencies and habits by establishing new ones. You can "round the peg" if you are sufficiently motivated. But before you achieve success in changing your tendencies and habits, be prepared to face mental and moral conflicts. You can win if you are willing to pay the price. You may find it difficult to pay each necessary installment—particularly the first few. But when you have paid in full, the newly established traits will predominate. The old tendencies and habits will become dormant. You will be happy because you will be doing what now comes naturally.

To guarantee success it is desirable that you try zealously to maintain physical, mental, and moral health during the period of such an internal struggle.

Points to Remember

1. Satisfaction is a mental attitude.
2. Opt for a job that comes naturally to you.
3. Use self-motivators such as: *I feel healthy! I feel happy! I feel terrific!* to motivate yourself to positive action in the desired direction.

11

THE 17 PRINCIPLES OF SUCCESS

The list that follows is meant to serve as a reminder. Look it over once a week. Are you making regular progress in each of these areas? If you routinely evaluate your efforts to embrace the principles, you are less likely to be caught in a crisis because you've neglected to think accurately, for instance, or to find that your coworkers suddenly regard you as an opportunistic shark.

1. Develop definiteness of purpose
2. Establish a mastermind alliance
3. Assemble an attractive personality
4. Use applied faith
5. Go the extra mile
6. Create personal initiative
7. Build a positive mental attitude
8. Control your enthusiasm
9. Enforce self-discipline
10. Think accurately
11. Control your attention
12. Inspire teamwork
13. Learn from adversity and defeat
14. Cultivate creative vision
15. Maintain sound health

16. Budget your time and money
17. Use cosmic habitforce

A DETAILED EVALUATION

Following are concise summaries of the steps to making each principle a part of your life. Read them through and then use the lines provided at the end of each section to write down specific actions you plan to take to implement the principles.

The summaries themselves will give you concrete recommendations about what to do. Under the definiteness of purpose you might write down that you will define your major goal, write out a plan for achieving it, and read that plan aloud to yourself every day, all of which are mentioned in the summary. But if you also include a date by which you will have your plan written down, you will be making a commitment to yourself that will provide you with extra motivation. So do not simply parrot back the summary's suggestions; consider carefully the changes you need to make and be as detailed as possible in writing them out. In a few weeks or months you can look at these notes, recognize the progress you've made, and renew your commitment to success.

1. Develop DEFINITENESS OF PURPOSE—with PMA

You should have one high, desirable, outstanding goal, and keep it ever before you. You can have many nonconflicting goals which help you to reach your major definite goal. It is advisable to have immediate, intermediate, and distant objectives. When you set a definite major goal, you are apt to recognize that which will help you achieve it.

Determine or fix in your mind exactly what you desire. Be definite.

Evaluate and determine exactly what you will give in return.

Set a definite date for exactly when you intend to possess your desire.

Identify your desire with a definite plan for carrying out and achieving your objective. Put your plan into action at once.

Clearly define your plan for achievement. Write out precisely and concisely exactly what you want, exactly when you want to achieve it, and exactly what you intend to give in return.

Each and every day, morning and evening, read your written statement aloud. As you read it, see, feel, and believe yourself already in possession of your objective.

Engage in personal inspection with regularity to determine whether you are on the right track and headed in the right direction so that you don't deviate from the path that leads to the achievement of your objective.

To guarantee success, engage daily in study, thinking, and planning time with PMA regarding yourself and your family and how you can achieve your definite goals.

WHATEVER YOUR MIND CAN CONCEIVE AND BELIEVE, YOU CAN ACHIEVE—WHEN YOU HAVE PMA AND APPLY IT.

My commitment to use this principle in my life is:

_____
_____
_____
_____

2. Establish A Mastermind Alliance—with PMA

A mastermind alliance is two or more minds working together in the spirit of perfect harmony toward the attainment of a specific objective.

This principle makes it possible for you, through association with others, to acquire and utilize the knowledge and experience needed for the attainment of any desired goal in

Your mastermind alliance can be created by surrounding yourself or aligning yourself with the advice, counsel, and personal cooperation of several people who are willing to lend you their wholehearted aid for the attainment of your objective in the spirit of perfect harmony.

You can create a mastermind alliance with your spouse, your manager, a friend, a coworker, etc. Once a mastermind alliance is formed, the group as a whole must become and remain active. The group must move in a definite plan, at a definite time, toward a definite common objective. Indecision, inactivity, or delay will destroy usefulness of the alliance. There must be a complete meeting of the minds without reservations on the part of any member.

You can have several mastermind alliances, each with different objectives—i.e., an alliance with your spouse to reach your family objectives, an alliance with your banker or investment counselor or attorney for your financial objectives, an alliance with your minister or clergy for your spiritual objectives, etc.

My commitment to use this principle in my life is:
_____
_____
_____
_____

3. Assemble an ATTRACTIVE PERSONALITY—with PMA

Your personality is your greatest asset or greatest liability, for it embraces everything that you control: mind, body, and soul. A person's personality is the person. It shapes the nature of your thoughts, your deeds, your relationships with others, and it establishes the boundaries of the space you occupy in the world.

It is essential that you develop a pleasing personality—pleasing to yourself and to others.

It is imperative that you develop the habit of being sensitive to your own reactions to individuals, circumstances, and events and to the reactions of individuals and groups to what you say, think, or do.

Positive Factors of a Pleasing Personality

- A positive mental attitude
- Tolerance
- Alertness
- Common courtesy
- A fondness for people
- Flexibility
- Tactfulness
- Personal magnetism
- A pleasant tone of voice
- Control of facial expressions
- Sportsmanship
- Sincerity
- A sense of humor
- Humility of the heart
- Smiling
- Enthusiasm Control of temper and emotions
- Patience

- Proper dress

DO UNTO OTHERS AS YOU WOULD HAVE OTHERS DO UNTO YOU.

My commitment to use this principle in my life is:
_____
_____
_____
_____

4. Use APPLIED FAITH—with PMA

Faith is a state of mind through which your aims, desires, plans, and purposes may be translated into their physical or financial equivalent.

Applied faith means action—specifically, the habit of applying your faith under any and all circumstances. It is faith in your God, yourself, your fellowman—and the unlimited opportunities available to you.

Faith without action is dead. Faith is the art of believing by doing. It comes as a result of persistent action. Fear and doubt are faith in reverse gear. Faith, in its positive application, is the key which will give one direct communications with Infinite Intelligence.

Applied faith is belief in an objective or purpose backed by unqualified activity. If you want results, try a prayer. When you pray, express your gratitude, and thanksgiving for the blessings you already have received; then ask the Good Lord for his help. Affirm the objectives of your desires through prayer each night and morning. Inspire your imagination to see yourself already in possession of them, and act precisely as if you were already in physical possession of them. The possession of anything first takes place mentally by being imagined in the mind's eye.

PRAYER IS YOUR GREATEST POWER!

My commitment to use this principle in my life is:

_____
_____
_____
_____

5. Go the EXTRA MILE—with PMA

Render more and better service for which you are paid, and do it with a positive mental attitude. Form the habit of going the extra mile because of the pleasure you get out of it and because of what it does to you and for you deep down inside. It is inevitable that every seed of useful service you sow will multiply itself and come back to you in overwhelming abundance.

Following this principle will make you indispensable to other people. The principle manifests itself in two important laws: the Law of Compensation and the Law of Increasing Returns. These unvarying laws always reward intelligent effort rendered in the attitude of faith and rendered instinctively without regards to the limits of immediate compensation.

$$Q^1 + Q^2 + MA = C$$

The quality of the service rendered plus the quantity of the service rendered plus the mental attitude in which it is rendered equals your compensation in the world and the amount of space you will occupy in the hearts of your fellow man.

MAKE GOING THE EXTRA MILE WITH PMA A HABIT!

My commitment to use this principle in my life is:

_____
_____

_____

_____

6. Create PERSONAL INITIATIVE—with PMA

Personal initiative is the inner power that starts all action. It is the power that inspires the completion of that which one begins. It is the dynamo that starts the faculty of the imagination into action.

It is, in fact, Self-motivation.

Motivation is that which induces action or determines choice. It is that which provides a motive. A motive is that inner urge only within the individual which incites you to action, such as an idea, an emotion, a desire, or an impulse. It is a hope or other force which starts in an attempt to produce specific results.

When you know principles that can motivate you, you will then know principles that can motivate others.

Motivate yourself with PMA. Hope is the magic ingredient in motivation, but the secret of accomplishment is getting into action.

USE AND DEVELOP THE SELF-STARTER. DO IT NOW!

My commitment to use this principle in my life is:

_____

_____

_____

_____

7. Build a POSITIVE MENTAL ATTITUDE

PMA stands for "positive mental attitude."

A positive mental attitude is the right, honest, constructive thought, action, or reaction to any person, situation, or set of circumstances that does not violate the laws of God or the right of one's fellowman.

PMA allows you to build on hope and overcome the negative attitudes of despair and discouragement. It gives you the mental power, the feeling, the confidence to do anything you make up your mind to do. PMA is commonly referred to as the "I can...I will" attitude applicable to all challenging circumstances in your life.

You create and maintain a positive mental attitude through your own willpower, based on motives of your own adaption. To develop PMA, strive to understand and apply the Golden Rule; be considerate and sensitive to the reactions of others; be sensitive to your own reactions by controlling your emotional responses; be a good finder; believe that any goal can be achieved; and develop what are understood to be right habits of thought and action.

A positive mental attitude is the catalyst necessary for achieving worthwhile success. Achievement is attained through some combination of PMA and definiteness of purpose with one or more of the other fifteen success principles.

MAINTAIN THE RIGHT ATTITUDE—A POSITIVE MENTAL ATTITUDE.

My commitment to use this principle in my life is:

_____
_____
_____
_____

8. Control Your Enthusiasm—with PMA

A person without enthusiasm is like a watch without a

mainspring. Father John O'Brien, research professor of theology at the University of Notre Dame, says, "the first ingredient which I believe is absolutely necessary for a successful, efficient, and competent individual is enthusiasm." He adds, "Enthusiasm comes from the Greek words that let you look into the root of this word—into its basic, fundamental and original meaning. The first is *theos*, which means God. The other two words are *en-Tae*, so that in the early usage of this term of the ancient Greeks, it literally meant, 'God within you.'" Further: "No battle of any importance can be won without enthusiasm."

To become enthusiastic about achieving a desirable goal, keep your mind on that goal day after day. The more worthy and desirable your objectives, the more dedicated and enthusiastic you will become. Understand and act on William James's statement: "The emotions are not always immediately subject to reason but they are always immediately subject to ACTION" (emphasis added). Enthusiasm thrives on a positive mind and positive action. This is the key to controlling your enthusiasm: always give it a worthy goal to focus on and once you have channeled it toward that goal, it will carry you forward.

Real enthusiasm comes from within. However, enthusiasm is like getting water from a well; first you have to prime the pump but soon the water flows and flows and flows. You can be enthusiastic about everything and anything you know or do. Enthusiasm is a PMA characteristic. It can be generated naturally from one's thoughts, feelings and emotions, but more important, it can be generated at will.

TO BE ENTHUSIASTIC... ACT ENTHUSIASTICALLY!

My commitment to use the principle in my life is:

_____

_____

_____
_____

9. Enforce SELF-DISCIPLINE—with PMA

Self-discipline enables you to develop control over yourself. Self-discipline begins with mastery of your thoughts, what you really are, what you really do. Your failures and your successes are the results of habits. We are creatures of habit, but because we are minds with bodies, we can change our habits.

Self-discipline is perhaps the most important function in aiding an individual in the development and maintenance of habits of thought which enable that person to fix his or her entire attention upon any desired purpose and to hold it there until that purpose has been attained.

If you do not control your thoughts, you do not control your deeds. Think first and act afterward. Self-discipline is the principle by which you may voluntarily shape the patterns of your thoughts to harmonize with your goals and purposes.

DIRECT YOUR THOUGHTS, CONTROL YOUR EMOTIONS, ORDAIN YOUR DESTINY WITH PMA.

My commitment to use this principle in my life is:

_____
_____
_____
_____

10. THINK ACCURATELY—with PMA

Accurate thinking is based on two major fundamentals:

1. Inductive reasoning, based on the assumption of unknown facts or hypotheses.

2. Deductive reasoning, based on known facts or what are believed to be facts.

In school we are taught deductive and inductive reasoning and the fallacy that results in starting with the wrong premise in the one instance and making the wrong inference in the other. Accurate thinking and common sense are in part the result of experiences. You can learn from your own experiences as well as those of others when you learn how to recognize, relate, assimilate, and apply principles in order to achieve your goals.

1. Separate facts from fiction or hearsay evidence.
2. Separate facts into classes: important and unimportant.

Be careful of others' opinions. They could be dangerous and destructive. Make sure your opinions are not someone else's prejudices. The accurate thinker learns to use his or her own judgment and to be cautious no matter who may endeavor to influence him or her.

TRUTH WILL BE TRUTH REGARDLESS OF A CLOSED MIND, IGNORANCE, OR REFUSAL TO BELIEVE.

My commitment to use this principle in my life is:
_____
_____
_____
_____

11. Control YOUR ATTENTION—with PMA

Controlled attention is organized mind power. It is the highest form of self-discipline. Controlled attention is the act of coordinating all the faculties of the mind and directing their combined power to a given end or definite objective. It is an act that can be obtained only by the strictest sort of self-discipline.

It is obvious, therefore, that when you voluntarily fix your attention upon a definite major purpose of a positive nature and force your mind through your daily habits of thought to dwell on the subject, you condition your subconscious mind to act on that purpose. Controlled attention, when it is focused upon the object of your definite major purpose, is a medium by which you make positive application of the principle of suggestion.

The mind never remains inactive, not even during sleep. It works continuously by reactions to the influences which reach it. Therefore, the object of controlled attention is that of keeping your mind busy with thought material which may be helpful in attaining the object of your desire.

Controlled attention is self-mastery of the highest order, for it is an accepted fact that the person who controls his or her own mind may control everything else.

KEEP YOUR MIND ON THE THINGS YOU WANT AND OFF THE THINGS YOU DON'T WANT.

My commitment to use this principle in my life is:

_____
_____
_____
_____

12. Inspire TEAMWORK—with PMA

Teamwork is a willing cooperation and the coordination of effort to achieve a specific objective. When the spirit of teamwork is willing, voluntary, and free, it leads to the attainment of great and enduring power.

It is a system which coordinates all the team players'

resources and talents and automatically discourages dishonesty and unfairness, while it adequately compensates the individuals who serve honestly and unselfishly.

The principle of teamwork differs from the mastermind principle in that it is based on the coordination of effort without necessarily embracing the principle of definiteness of purpose or the principle of harmony, two important essentials of the mastermind.

Teamwork produces power, but the question of whether the power is temporary or permanent depends on the motive that inspired the cooperation. If the motive is one that inspires people to cooperate willingly, the power produced by this sort of teamwork will endure as long as that spirit of willingness prevails.

Teamwork builds individuals and businesses and provides unlimited opportunity for all. It is sharing a part of what you have—a part that is good—with others.

THAT WHICH YOU SHARE WILL MULTIPLY; THAT WHICH YOU WITHHOLD WILL DIMINISH.

My commitment to use this principle in my life is:

_____
_____
_____
_____

13. Learn from ADVERSITY AND DEFEAT—with PMA

Every adversity carries with it the seed of an equivalent or greater benefit for those who have PMA and apply it.

Defeat may be a stepping-stone or a stumbling block, according to your mental attitude and how you relate it to yourself.

It is never the same as failure unless and until it has been accepted as such.

Your mental attitude in respect to defeat is the factor of major importance which determines whether you ride with tides of fortune or misfortune. The person with a positive metal attitude reacts to defeat in the spirit of determination not to accept it. The person with a negative mental attitude reacts to defeat in the spirit of hopeless acceptance.

THE WORST THING THAT HAPPENS TO YOU MAY BE THE BEST THING THAT CAN HAPPEN TO YOU IF YOU DON'T LET IT GET THE BEST OF YOU.

My commitment to use this principle in my life is:

14. Cultivate CREATIVE VISION—with PMA

Man's greatest gift is his thinking mind. It analyzes, compares, chooses. It creates, visualizes, foresees, and generates ideas.

Imagination is your mind's exercise, challenge, and adventure. It is the key to all of a person's achievements, the mainspring of all human endeavor, the secret door to the soul of a person. Imagination inspires human endeavor in connection with material things and ideas associated with material things.

Imagination is the workshop of the human mind, where old ideas and established facts may be assembled into new combinations and put to new uses. It is the act of constructive intellect in the grouping of materials, knowledge, or thoughts into new, original, and rational systems, a constructive or creative faculty embracing poetic, artistic, philosophical, scientific, and ethical imagination.

Creative vision may be an inborn quality of the mind or an acquired quality, for it may be developed by the free and fearless use of the faculty of imagination.

Creative vision extends beyond interest in material things. It judges the future by the past and concerns itself with the future more than with the past. Imagination is influenced and controlled by the powers of reason and experience. Creative vision pushes these aside and attains its ends by basically new ideas and methods.

One of the ways to increase your flow of ideas is by developing the habit of taking study time, thinking time, and planning time. Be quiet and motionless, and listen for that small, still voice that speaks from within as you contemplate the ways in which you can achieve your objectives.

WHAT CAN BE CONCEIVED CAN BE CREATED—WITH PMA.

My commitment to use this principle in my life is:

_____
_____
_____
_____

15. Maintain SOUND HEALTH—with PMA

You are a mind with a body. Inasmuch as your brain controls your body, recognize that sound physical health demands a positive mental attitude, a health consciousness. Establish good, well-balanced health habits in work, play, rest, nourishment, and study. To maintain a health consciousness, think in terms of good physical health, not in terms of illness or disease. Remember, what your mind focuses upon, your mind brings into existence, whether it is financial success or physical health.

To maintain a positive attitude for the development and

maintenance of a sound health consciousness, use self-discipline, keep your mind free of negative thoughts and influence, and create and maintain a well-balanced life. Follow work with play, mental effort with physical effort, seriousness with humor, and you will be on the road to good health and happiness.

A sound mind and a sound body are attainable if you will put PMA to work for you. Remember, you can enjoy good health and live longer with PMA.

I FEEL HEALTHY! I FEEL HAPPY! I FEEL TERRIFIC!

My commitment to use this principle in my life is:

_____
_____
_____
_____

16. Budget your TIME AND MONEY—with PMA

Intelligently balance your use of time and resources, both business and personal. Take inventory of yourself and your activities so that you discover where and how you are spending your time and your money.

Engage in study, thinking, and planning time.

Don't waste your time or your money. Ten percent of all you earn is yours to keep and invest. Like any good business, budget your money. Use your time wisely toward attainment of your objectives. Develop a plan for the use of your income for expenses, savings, and investments.

YOU DON'T ALWAYS GET WHAT YOU EXPECT UNLESS YOU INSPECT—WITH PMA.

My commitment to use this principle in my life is:

17. Use cosmic HABITFORCE—with PMA

Cosmic habitforce pertains to the entire universe and is the law by which the equilibrium of the universe is maintained through established patterns or habits. It is the law which forces every living creature and every particle of matter to come under the dominating influence of its environment, including the physical habits and thought habits of humankind.

Cosmic habitforces are the powers which you apply with PMA when you use the universal laws or principles. Cosmic habitforces are employed when you use your mind powers whether they pertain to your conscious or subconscious mind. That is how you think and grow richer or achieve anything in life you desire (in principle) that doesn't violate the laws of God or the rights of your fellowman.

All of us are ruled by habits. These are fastened upon us by repeated thoughts and experiences. You have complete right of control over your thoughts. We create patterns of thought by repeating certain ideas or behavior until the Law of Cosmic Habitforce takes over those patterns and makes them more or less permanent unless or until you consciously rearrange them.

Habits: You have them—some good, perhaps others bad. Many you are aware of, but some that are undesirable you are blinded to. Each begins in your mind consciously or subconsciously. And each can be developed and neutralized or changed at will through the proper use of your mind. You have this power.

You are ruled by your habits. It takes a habit to replace a habit. Develop positive habits that will be in harmony with the achievement of your definite purpose or goal.

SOW AN ACT, AND YOU REAP A HABIT.
SOW A HABIT, AND YOU REAP A CHARACTER.
SOW A CHARACTER, AND YOU REAP A DESTINY.

My commitment to use this principle in my life is:

_____
_____
_____
_____

Points to Remember

1. Determine or fix in your mind exactly what you desire. Be definite.
2. Create mastermind alliances.
3. It is essential to develop a pleasing personality.

www.ingramcontent.com/pod-product-compliance
Lightning Source LLC
Chambersburg PA
CBHW030219170426
43194CB00007BA/791